1065 BROADWAY

$107. tuition

The Berkshire Studies in European History

GENERAL EDITORS

RICHARD A. NEWHALL
LAURENCE B. PACKARD
SIDNEY R. PACKARD

Berkshire Studies in European History

Under the Editorship of
Richard A. Newhall, Laurence B. Packard
and Sidney R. Packard

THE
INDUSTRIAL REVOLUTION

BY

FREDERICK C. DIETZ
ASSOCIATE PROFESSOR OF HISTORY
UNIVERSITY OF ILLINOIS

NEW YORK
HENRY HOLT AND COMPANY

PREFACE

The college teacher of general European history is always confronted with the task of finding adequate reading for his classes which is neither too specialized and technical nor too elementary. For many topics, including several of the greatest importance, no such material is at the moment available. Moreover, in too many instances, good reading which undeniably does exist is in the form of a chapter in a larger work and is therefore too expensive for adoption as required reading under normal conditions.

The Berkshire Studies in European History have been planned to meet this situation. The topics selected for treatment are those on which there is no easily accessible reading of appropriate length adequate for the needs of a course in general European history. The authors, all experienced teachers, are in nearly every instance actively engaged in the class room and intimately acquainted with its problems. They will avoid a merely elementary presentation of facts, giving instead an interpretive discussion suited to the more mature point of view of college students.

No pretense is made, of course, that these *Studies* are contributions to historical literature in the scholarly sense. Each author, nevertheless, is sufficiently a specialist in the period of which he writes to be familiar with the sources and to have used the latest scholarly contributions to his subject. In order that those who desire to read further on any topic may have some guidance short bibliographies of works in western European languages are given, with particular attention to books of recent date.

Each *Study* is designed as a week's reading. The division into three approximately equal chapters, many of them self-contained and each suitable for one day's assignment, should make the series as a whole easily adaptable to the present needs of college classes. The editors have attempted at every point to maintain and emphasize this fundamental flexibility.

Maps and diagrams will occasionally be furnished with the text when specially needed but a good historical atlas, such as that of Shepherd, is presupposed throughout.

R. A. N.
L. B. P.
S. R. P.

CONTENTS

THE INDUSTRIAL
REVOLUTION

CHAPTER I

THE ROOTS OF THE INDUSTRIAL REVOLUTION

EUROPEAN LIFE IN THE MIDDLE OF THE EIGHTEENTH CENTURY

In its social and economic aspects the European scene before the middle of the eighteenth century presented features which are distinctly different from those of the twentieth century.

In contrast with the teeming populations of today, the whole continent was sparsely occupied. England, which now supports forty million people, did not yet count six and a half million heads. Prussia, including the newly won province of Silesia, had about three and a half million inhabitants; Austria, six million; and France, the most populous state in western Europe, nineteen millions. Not only was the population small, but until just before 1750 its rate of growth had been so extremely slow that Gregory King, an English statistician of the beginning of the eighteenth century, estimated that, in the case of his own country, the number of the people would not reach eleven million until the year 2300. In Württemberg, one of the most densely settled of the German principalities, the increase was about 27 per cent between 1700 and 1750; in England, 17 or 18 per cent. In the small countries, such as Norway, the growth was less rapid.

Town life was, of course, already well developed, and many cities had long and stirring histories. Before 1789 France could boast of seventy-nine cities of more than ten thousand inhabitants, some of which went back a thousand years. Paris, the largest capital in Europe, numbered nearly seven hundred thousand people, and London, only slightly smaller, was soon to surpass it in size. Amsterdam, Vienna, Naples, Palermo, and Rome stood between one and two hundred thousand; many of the smaller territorial capitals and commercial centers, such as Bristol, Copenhagen, Dantzig, and Geneva ranged from twenty to one hundred thousand. The prolific industrial centers of modern times, Essen, Manchester, Birmingham, Creusot, and others, were still country villages or were just beginning their mushroom development. Manchester already had 40,000 people, Birmingham 30,000, and Sheffield 30,000, although each of these places had had only about 4,000 inhabitants in 1700.

In 1750 towns were still either political capitals, enlivened by the presence of the prince and his bureaucrats and soldiers, and supported by the surplus wealth of the country which flowed in under the form of taxes; commercial depots, favorably situated for international trade; or the *foci* of the local business life of the small, more or less separate economic areas into which Europe was still divided. One town might, of course, be two or even all three of these things, as London was, for example. Here, as in other capitals, the ostentation and

extravagance of court life supported large numbers of
artisans and tradesmen engaged in the luxury trades.
To meet the expenses of following the fashions, moreover, the nobles had to think of increasing their rev-
enues; and while they often sought to do this through
securing government sinecures, very frequently they
were led to initiate improvements in agriculture on their
estates in order that they might raise their rents.

The higher standards of living at court, which reached
their apogee at Versailles, affected every group of the
population. They were based, to a large extent, upon
the use of new products of colonial origin, such as
chocolate, tea, coffee, sugar, spices, dye-woods, tobacco,
silks, calicoes, jewels, fine furniture, china ware, oriental
rugs, slaves, and furs; and the favorable situation for
trade in these articles of certain ancient cities, such as
Amsterdam, London, Bristol, and Lisbon, gave to their
merchants the opportunity of building up important
overseas trades, organized under the form of such companies as the Dutch East India Company, the Hudson's
Bay Company, and the French Guinea Company.
These enriched their respective communities not only
through the importation of the valuable American or
Asiatic products, but through export and sale of such
wares all over Europe. So profitable was the business
that the merchants of every country sought to gain exclusive privileges and monopolies for themselves in such
regions as the fur producing area of America, the silk
and fine textile districts of India, and the spice growing islands of the East Indies; and by 1750 the wars
for the control of these " colonies " had not yet been

concluded. More than that, to pay the colonial producers for their wares, European goods were exported;
and the development in Africa, Asia, and America of
markets for British, French, and Dutch manufactures
was one of the most important reactions of the whole
procedure.

Still another kind of business accounted for the extent and prosperity of the towns in the eighteenth
century. Certain districts of Europe were naturally
adapted for the production of certain commodities.
Portugal was especially suitable for wine growing; in
Lincolnshire, and in other counties in England, sheep
abounded. While wool was not manufactured into cloth
in London, entrepreneurs of the city had organized, or
secured control of, the manufacture of cloth in Norfolk,
Essex, Yorkshire, and in the southwest counties; and,
under the protection of favorable trade treaties, they
proceeded to exchange English cloth for port wine, to
the enrichment of themselves and the advantage of their
city. The Dutch imported large quantities of grain
from the Baltic to make good their own deficiencies;
herring, pitch, timber, rope and cordage, and iron were
likewise exchanged between those countries which had
a surplus and those which had a shortage.

As a consequence of the growth of European cities in
the period before 1750, it was necessary for them to
reach farther and farther into the country districts for
their food supplies, fuel, the raw materials used by
their craftsmen, and especially for the cheap labor supply of the more remote places which formed so important an element in the manufacture of woolen cloth

and other articles for export. In this way certain cities came to dominate the life of whole districts, and Europe was, early in the eighteenth century, more truly divided into metropolitan areas, more or less separate from each other, than into political states. There was a certain amount of recognition of this in the Germanies, where the small political principality and the metropolitan economic area were much the same thing. The cities set the tone of the life of the region which they controlled, and kept it in touch with the latest developments in taste and fashion.

In spite of the leavening influence of the cities on the life which surrounded them, it must always be kept in mind that, measured by modern standards, their trade was exceedingly small. The tonnage cleared outward from all English ports in 1750 was only 660,000 tons, and seventy years later (1820) that entering French ports was only slightly larger, 690,000 tons, ten or eleven times the tonnage of a single modern ship like the *Leviathan* or *Berengaria*.

As a corollary to a scanty commerce there was limited manufacturing of articles for sale or exchange. The total iron production in England in 1740 was only 17,-350 tons; the value of woolen cloth produced was gradually rising to " full four millions "; and 2,976,000 pounds weight of raw cotton were imported. Perhaps it is not altogether fair to use some of these figures as indices of industry in 1750, since neither cotton nor iron manufactures were nearly so significant as linen, wooden ware, and leather, for which figures are lacking. It must be remembered, too, that home industry

was very wide-spread.   Many families made all their
own textiles, leather, furniture, and other commodities.

In view of the limited character of business it is not
surprising that methods of production and distribution
were less highly complicated than today.   Wholesale
trade with foreign parts was, in many branches of business, highly developed.   In England the great merchants, either as individuals or as organized companies,
such as the East India Company, were considerably
more significant than they were on the continent; and
they exercised an exceptional influence in politics and
foreign affairs.   Yet this consideration must not ob-
scure the fact that even in England the total of overseas trade was slight, and relatively unimportant in
comparison with internal trade.

In certain branches of wholesale domestic business,
such as the grain trade, a series of middlemen between
the producer and consumer had developed, and a good
deal was known of the commercial salesman and the
factor or commission merchant.

Retail trade was small in bulk, and, generally speak-
ing, a humble business everywhere.   In 1745 London
had shops on which " in excess of £500 " was spent for
decorations, fine shelves, shutters, glass windows, and
columns, but there were only a few shopping streets
even in the largest cities; in the smaller towns there
were only " general stores " which sold everything from
sugar and coffee to calico and candles in an unglazed,
dirt-floored room; and in many places there were no
shops at all.   The weekly market, the semi-annual fair,
and the itinerant peddler or chapman were the regular

channels of distribution of the great bulk of such goods
as had to be purchased. It was not until eighty or a
hundred years later (1830–50) that the little shops of
mercers and spicers in Paris began their development
into the great business establishments of modern times,
when such men as M. Parissot added ready made clothing to his needles, calico, and tape, and M. Thernaux
employed tailors and seamstresses to work for him on
dresses and suits to be sold ready made in his shop at
the sign of *Bonhomme Richard, Place des Victoires*.

In the organization of industry the employment of
considerable capital was of course a marked feature
long before the middle of the eighteenth century. The
direction and control of manufacturing was very generally in the hands of an entrepreneur, who owned the
materials and tools and understood the problems of securing raw materials and finding markets, and thus
stood between the producer of raw materials, the workers, and the consumer. There were many instances
where this condition did not exist, where independent
master-craftsmen worked as they did in the Middle
Ages for direct sale to the consumers; and although
such craftsmen continued to play a rôle far into the
nineteenth century in Germany, for example, they were
the exception rather than the rule.

The presence of the capitalist entrepreneur was not
incompatible with the continuance of medieval gilds,
with their systems of mastership and apprenticeship,
and in 1750 gilds were not only legal everywhere in
western Europe, but on the continent they still continued to function. In France they were destroyed by

the Revolution; in many parts of Germany they survived into the nineteenth century. In England, on the other hand, where they were not legally abolished until 1835, they were already declining in importance in the eighteenth century, and no new gilds were organized for new trades as these developed.

The term generally applied to describe eighteenth century industrial organization is the Domestic System. It can be illustrated best by reference to the English cloth manufacture in the southwestern counties. Here the entrepreneurs were known as the clothiers, who often amassed fortunes of as much as £10,000 and even £20,000. They bought the raw wool directly in the periodical wool markets either in London or in Cirencester, and then delivered it weekly among spinners, who lived in the vicinity of the little clothing towns. When the yarn was collected on the clothier's next round, it was carried to weavers, who worked in their own cottages, at piecework rates, on looms which were probably the property of the clothier. The cloth was now collected and sent to London by wagon trains to be sold through factors at Blackwell Hall to the export merchants or retail tailors, or exported by way of Bristol or other western ports. So complete was the dependence of the workers on the clothier, that when a clothier of Tiverton died, the workers petitioned the mayor of Tiverton to bring in another in his place, lest they be forced to starve from lack of work.

In the north of England more independence remained to the workers. The weavers, scattered about through the country, working in their own cottages to each of which a small garden was attached, were masters of their own tools and materials; they purchased their supplies in London and either carried their finished cloth in the white to market in the local towns, such as Leeds or Bradford, where it was purchased by export merchants, or sent it to London by common carriers to be sold.

This system in both its "putting out" and "cottage" forms recommended itself to the workers because it left them "free." They could work when and how they pleased without supervision, and they could bring in their families to assist them. The entrepreneur had little fixed capital invested, and when slack times came, he could withdraw from industry without much loss, and with the consciousness that, owing to the by-employments made possible by the possession of garden plots, the workers were not starving. This knowledge also helped him to beat down piecework rates, while the dispersal of the workers made it impossible for them to take much common action to protect themselves from wage reductions or from payment in truck. One clothier once took advantage of a glut in the pepper market to purchase great supplies of pepper, which he insisted that his workers accept in payment of their wages. To revenge themselves for such treatment domestic workers habitually stole part of the material entrusted to them, and legislation was never able to extirpate either the theft of materials or payment in truck. Parliamentary statutes continued to be enacted and penalties were made more severe, but the evils remained unabated through the whole of the eighteenth century.

RURAL LIFE IN 1750

In spite of the urban development associated with commerce and industry the population of Europe was still predominantly rural in 1750. Even in France not more than 21 or 22 per cent of the people lived in cities, and while the percentage was higher in England, due to the existence of London, it was probably lower on the rest of the continent. Agriculture was the chief occupation of the overwhelming majority of the people; and, in a very general way, little surplus for sale or exchange was produced by the ordinary farmer or peasant. He raised his own food and the materials for his clothing, such as wool, linen, and leather, and secured his material for building, furniture, and fuel from the communal waste or forest.

At the same time he had already long since felt the corroding desire for brooches and rings, mirrors and lace and silk, combs and pins, pewter cups and such other trinkets, which could be purchased from the traveling peddler only for money. To secure the money the agriculturalist might take advantage of the market of the neighboring town and produce a certain surplus for sale there, or he might allow himself or his wife and children to be drawn into the orbit of town industry as rural domestic workers. Nevertheless, it was still true in many parts of Europe that there had been little change in agricultural life since the Middle Ages. Except in England, Flanders, and Holland, no new crops had as yet been introduced, and in vast stretches of Europe personal serfdom still continued legally in force.

THE ISOLATION OF EUROPEAN LIFE

Perhaps the most significant characteristic of European life in this period, which serves to explain the backwardness of the agricultural areas and the meagerness of commerce and industry was the isolation of districts from each other. So slight was communication between places and so seldom were strangers seen that when they did come to the more remote villages the people ran or shouted after them or even set dogs on them. Chiefly responsible for this condition was the wretched state of the roads, or their complete absence. Holland, it is true, had admirable waterways, and smooth highways paved with brick; France and Italy had preserved the Roman roads, and in France these had been added to and improved through the seventeenth century. Louis XV early in his reign created a *corps des Ponts et Chaussées* which put the roads of France into such excellent condition that Arthur Young spoke in superlatives of the best French roads: " stupendous works," " truly magnificent," " we have not an idea of what such a road is in England." East of the Rhine, however, roads scarcely existed; the so-called Army and Trade Roads of Germany were mere rights of way, and it was not until 1753 that the first paved road was constructed in Germany. Prussia did not begin to build any such roads until 1788.

In England something was already being done to make the mud tracks passable for horses in all seasons, but vehicles were still rare on the roads in 1750. Nevertheless, within a few years Warrington's Flying Coach was making the journey from Manchester to London in four and a half days, and the demand for better roads from scores of other coach proprietors and wagon-train owners led to the creation of turnpike trusts in very large numbers to repair and rebuild the English roads. Yet as late as 1792 it was stated in a private letter written in England that in the winter, when the cheerless season invited and required good fellowship, the intercourse of neighbors could not be kept up without imminent danger to life and limb.

To the physical barriers of evil roads were added political and legal obstacles to reduce communication, correspondence, and transport to a minimum. Every country was surrounded by high tariff walls ostensibly to aid in making the nation self-sufficient and independent of the outside world, but in reality to give protection to certain influential manufacturing and agricultural interests at home. Except in England the whole apparatus of medieval river tolls further burdened free mobility. Thus as late as 1800 on the Elbe between Hamburg and Magdeburg a cargo paid toll fourteen times, and on the Main, between Bamberg and Mainz, thirty-three times. In the sphere of personal freedom of movement, the obligations of serfdom kept a large part of the population tied to the soil on the continent, and in England the same effect was achieved by the Restoration Act of Settlement, which, still in force, practically prevented the agricultural laborers from leaving the villages in which they were born. To grow and die and rot in a single spot was most men's career.

THE BREAKING DOWN OF ISOLATION, AND THE ACCELERATION OF THE SPEED OF LIVING AFTER 1750

Into this rather sluggish, isolated social life of Europe various changes intruded themselves in the century after 1750 with apparent dramatic suddenness, although closer examination indicates that each new factor was but the cumulative effect of earlier, scarcely noticed developments. Among the most significant of the new phenomena was a remarkable increase in the population, in which every country participated. England went up by 52 per cent to over nine million inhabitants from 1750 to 1801 and reached thirty-six million in 1910. France added seven million to her population in the half century 1750–1800, and then grew more slowly to thirty-nine million in 1910. The territories which constitute modern Germany had twenty-four and one-half million people in 1801, and jumped to sixty-five million in 1910.

Closely connected with this extraordinary growth of the number of people in Europe there was apparently a sharp fall in the death-rate. It was less that more people were born per 1000 of the population, although this did take place to a very limited extent, but that fewer died in infancy and youth, that more lived to maturity, and that those who attained adult years continuously added to the normal span of life. So great has been the effect of the lengthening of life in the most recent past that even though the birth-rate has fallen sharply in every country in western Europe the growth of population still continues, even though only very slowly in the case of such nations as France.

The reasons for the decline in the death-rate in the period after 1750 are not altogether understood. In England where the growth was more spectacular than in any other country in the century 1750–1850 something must be attributed to the restrictions on gin drinking, which became effective in 1751, and still more to the growing belief that bad conditions and high mortality were not due to original sin or to the designs of an inscrutable Providence, but to evil laws and bad environment. In the worst years before 1750, 74 per cent of the children born in London died before they were five years old, and 80 per cent of all parish children died. Owing to the work of Jonas Hanway and the Foundling Hospital these figures were sharply reduced, and while the death-rate of children was still high, something was being done to spread a knowledge of the proper care of infants.

Another important departure was the study of midwifery and the foundation of lying-in or maternity hospitals after 1747, which, before the end of the century, reduced the deaths from 1 in 42 to 1 in 913 among the mothers, and from 1 in 15 to 1 in 115 among the newborn babies. Of more general importance was the discovery of innoculation for smallpox by Hunter in 1740 and the establishment of vaccination by Jenner in 1798; and in the beginning of the nineteenth century typhus fever, which was perennially epidemic in large cities, was finally brought under control.

Much was gained, too, by the practice of greater

cleanliness and ventilation which came into use in the hospitals after 1783 and spread slowly among the population, and by the dispensary movement which began in London in 1769 to bring medical advice within the reach of the poor. Changes in fashions, moreover, made for greater hygiene. In the third quarter of the eighteenth century the wives of journeymen, tradesmen, and shopkeepers wore leather stays or corsets which were never washed, although worn every day for years; and the wives and grown daughters of all classes wore woolen petticoats, lined with linen, stuffed with wool and horsehair, and quilted, which were put on daily until they were rotten. The fashion of wearing easily washed cotton goods which presently came in made cleanliness possible as it had never been before.

The advance of medical science is probably only part of the explanation of the new population figures. There seems to be an intimate connection between population and subsistence; and, although it is popularly believed that population tends to encroach on the limits of subsistence, it is also possible that the emphasis should be the other way, and that an augmentation in subsistence possibilities may lead to a growth of the population. Easier conditions of living make it possible to rear more children and give them day by day such clothing, food, shelter, and hygienic conditions as will insure a sound and healthy physique. Under such circumstances medicine is only an emergency measure, and the real factor is the good health and general wellbeing made possible by the presence of sufficient large, easily attained subsistence supplies.

Certain facts are unquestionably established for the period after 1750. The first of these is an increase in the supply of food and essential materials, and the second is the rise in effective demand for supplies by all classes. It is not possible to speak categorically about the reaction of the two phenomena on each other, but there was probably a series of actions and reactions under the influence of which increased supplies of food and materials led to larger populations, and growing numbers of people stimulated food and supply production.

Some of the most significant developments in the augmentation of the supply of the basic materials of life in the eighteenth century came through the colonization of hitherto backward areas, such as the northern and western counties of England, and the settlement of the various European colonies on the American mainland and in the West Indies. The exploitation of the sugar plantations in the British and French West Indies, for example, added enormously to the existing food supplies of Europe. Sugar represented in a concentrated form not only the produce of the West Indies, but also, indirectly, a large part of the fish and grain of the colonies on the mainland, which were sold in the sugar islands to feed the plantation slaves.

As a denser population developed at home, its consuming power reacted to stimulate internal production. In the case of English agriculture, for example, the demand for food led to the alteration of the medieval field systems and the abolition of common rights wherever they still remained, so that improved methods and crops could be introduced. New machines, such as drills, harrows, and horse hoes, were invented; clover and turnips, brought over from Holland, did away with the fallow; and the intensive use of fertilizers turned extensive districts which had long produced nothing but "nettles and warrens" into "smiling cornfields."

Since meat was coming to be more valuable than powers of draft in an ox, or than wool in sheep, experiments in breeding began, with a view to producing animals in which such useless points as the longest legs or horns which fell back so that the ear showed in front were disregarded, and the heaviest weight of meat attained. On the best cultivated estates the wall-sided cattle, more like ill-made black horses "than an ox or a cow," and the sheep, with skins rattling on their bones like skeletons bound in parchment, were replaced by such new breeds of cattle as the Durham shorthorns, the Herefords, and the Devons, and such new breeds of sheep as the Leicesters.

The cumulative effect of all these changes can be illustrated by a few figures. Through the rearrangements of the fields four and one-half million acres of waste land were added to the cultivable area; the total produce of an average village of 4000 acres was raised from £5060 to £6600 in value; and the average size of beeves brought to the Smithfield market between 1710 and 1795 increased from 370 to 800 pounds, and of sheep from 28 to 80 pounds.

In the involved process of introducing the use of the new supplies, there was one very important step. This was in evidence when wheaten bread and meat became more common on the tables of Englishmen in the second half of the eighteenth century, but it was especially significant in connection with the more popular consumption of sugar and similar goods, since, chronologically considered, these were the materials which changed the European equilibrium of earlier periods. In common parlance people added sugar to their diets by buying it. This might have involved merely the spending of money for sugar which had been used to purchase other food, but the general development seems to have been not that sugar was substituted for other food, but that it was an addition to the normal standard of living, as were chocolate, tea, furs, silks, and other materials of colonial origin. To add new requisites to normal consumption it was necessary for the ordinary man to " increase his earnings," or, in other words, to work harder to add to his own production powers, so as to create other goods, perhaps manufactured articles, which might be exchanged in the last analysis for sugar and colonial wares.

The settlement and exploitation of the colonial world by Europeans, then, not only provided at least one of the prerequisites for a larger population, but it further made possible the satisfaction of that almost instinctive impulse among men to raise their living standards. In consequence there was everywhere in Europe a very rapid rise in tastes and requirements.

Among the upper classes in England where the new manifestation was earliest widespread, it took the form among the nobility of the erection of magnificent town and country houses furnished by the master furniture makers and designers, Chippendale, Sheraton, Heppel-white, and the brothers Adam, decorated by Angelica Kaufmann, and hung with portraits by Reynolds and Gainsborough. Many a lordly mansion had an almost international fame for the fountains, summer houses, and vistas of its park, and for the art treasures of its magnificent rooms and galleries.

The luxury of the aristocracy was aped by the classes below them, and even the "poor," whose standards were so inelastic as to call forth denunciation by the censors of morals because they would not work more than four days a week, but "sot or idle away their time," seem to have added potatoes, beets, carrots, and cabbages to their diets, and cotton and linen clothing to their wardrobes.

The psychological alertness and general quickening of activity indicated by this, as by any, rise in living standards was so noticeable that one contemporary observer was led to write in 1767: "Everything wears the face of dispatch. Dispatch, which is the very life and soul of business, becomes daily more attainable by the free circulation in every channel which is adapted to it." What he meant to indicate was that as a result of the speeding up and greater effort in the business of living, the isolation of former times was being broken down.

The development of mining, localized in the nature of things, made it necessary to open up communications with the consuming areas; the growth of cities sent merchants far afield in search of food supplies; and industrial entrepreneurs went further into the country to find their operatives. In many districts, especially in

England and France, there was the greatest activity in road building, and in the larger towns the inns served as depots for wagon trains and stage coaches. These " flying machines " already rattled along at four or five miles an hour or twenty leagues (sixty miles) a day, and, before so very long, in 1784, Palmer, the postmaster general, put on the mail coaches which ran without halting for the night and covered the remarkable distance of one hundred and twenty miles in a day of twenty-four hours.

For heavy goods traffic the canal was of greater importance than the road. France already gloried in the Canal de Languedoc, connecting the Atlantic with the Mediterranean, which moved Arthur Young to exclaim, " here Louis XIV thou art truly great "; and under Louis XVI she resumed work on the Canal of Picardy, which had been halted because of the expense of the tunneling works between St. Quentin and Cambrai. In 1759 the jilted Duke of Bridgewater began the first significant canal in England, to bring coal from his mines at Worsley to Manchester; and, before the century ended, the new industrial towns of the north and west were connected with each other and linked with London by an intricate network of canals. Over them coal came to Manchester and the blast furnaces of the west at onefourth the former cost, the Potteries imported their clay from Cornwall and sent out their delicate teacups and vases for export all over the world, emigrants found cheap access to the newly opened districts of the north, and the new towns were supplied with abundant food and cheap building material.

ENGLAND'S LEADERSHIP IN THE INDUSTRIAL REVOLUTION

Everywhere in consequence of the growth of the population, the rise in the standards of living, the settlement of new areas and the building of new towns, the construction of roads and canals, and the provision of goods for the colonial trades, there was the greatest activity in manufacture. This was true in France, Holland, and England particularly, but the extraordinary development of industry which followed was preëminently English.

In the first place, Great Britain had come out the victor in the great wars for colonial empire. For many years her merchants enjoyed the lucrative monopoly of the slave trade of Spanish America; and, when that monopoly was voided in 1750, Liverpool and Bristol free traders continued to supply the Spanish planters with their slaves in defiance of the Spanish law. In the West Indies Britain controlled many of the sugar islands, together with the mainland from which the islands were fed; and, even though the thirteen colonies presently won their political freedom, they remained economically dependent. England's armies drove the French from the fur-bearing area of America and strengthened her hold on the Newfoundland fishing banks. India, except for a few minor stations which had been left to France, had become the province of the British East India Company, and even China extended certain privileges of trade, which the Company exercised. England thus was in a position to experience the most effective reactions from colonial trade and supplies, and presently certain industries, such as the cotton industry, found themselves unable to meet the demands for goods made upon them unless fundamental changes in organization and technique were made.

The second factor in England's leadership was the Revolution of 1789 in France, followed before very long by the outbreak of war which involved the whole continent. Amidst the march of armies, the conscription of soldiers, encampments, battles, blockades, and the general confusion of economic life, European industry flagged; while Great Britain, unscathed by the destruction of war, not only supplied the needs of the continent and of the armies of Europe, including France, but in 1810 secured free entry into the markets of the South American republics, which had proclaimed their independence of Spain. It is almost impossible to overemphasize the impetus given to British industry by the events of the Revolutionary and Napoleonic wars. It was so great that in comparison with the feverish haste of business after 1793, an early nineteenth century economist could speak of the preceding decade, which was itself a period of remarkable growth, as " this tranquil condition, this medium between activity and stagnation."

CHANGES IN TECHNIQUE AND ORGANIZATION

The story of the technical progress of the first period of the Industrial Revolution is therefore the story of British developments, although even here certain achievements of Frenchmen and other Europeans cannot be omitted. When the English manufacturers of cotton goods found it hard to fill their orders with their present forces of domestic workers, they could not, like the *Verleger* of Saxony, go further into the country and draw more workers into the industry. The limited extent of the area in Lancashire and Cheshire where the climate was moist enough for cotton spinning, and the sparseness of the population rendered a repetition of what had already been done in the woolen cloth trades impossible.

In their quandary the cotton manufacturers turned to the idea of machinery, particularly for spinning, with which certain experiments had already been made, and in the 1760's the Society of Arts and Manufactures offered prizes for a practical machine to spin yarn. Under such incentives various types of spinning machines were invented and perfected in the next generation. One of these, the spinning jenny, was admirably suited for cottage work; and, with its wide introduction, the domestic system was given a new vitality and was able to meet the requirements for cotton yarn for many years. Other spinning machines, the water frame and the mule, were so large and heavy that they could not be used except where power was available, and their perfection and extended use after about 1788 made the continuance of the domestic system in the spinning of cotton yarn impossible.

At a very early date attention was also paid to the problem of weaving by machinery; and, although a mechanical loom was actually invented, it still needed so many refinements that it had little economic significance before the end of the Napoleonic wars. As the output of machine-made yarns increased, weavers were gathered from all parts of England and from Ireland to work in sheds, barns, lumber-rooms, cart-houses, and cottages in the villages adjacent to the yarn manufacturing centers; and weavers worked under the domestic system until the beginning of the second quarter of the nineteenth century.

The new heavy machines, such as the water frame, which first relied on horses or water wheels, presently encountered the problem of mechanical power, which had, however, long since risen in the tin and coal mines. As the shafts in the mines were driven to lower levels, much water was encountered. In Germany similar problems were solved by increasing the number of men on the pumps; but Cornwall and Northumberland had no surplus men for this sort of work, while the use of horses was prohibitive in cost on account of the shortage in fodder.

As early as 1698 a " fire engine " for pumping was invented, but it was only an interesting mechanical toy until its ideas were reincorporated into a more practicable motor by Newcomen in 1705–1711. His " Miner's Friend," with its cylinder from four to six feet in diameter and its piston making from six to twelve strokes a minute, was widely used not only in mines, but in waterworks and in blast furnaces, where the power was transmitted by pumping water to higher levels whence it fell over waterwheels attached to the blast pumps. In 1775, one hundred and thirty of these motors were in use; but the largest types delivered only about twenty horse power with a coal consumption of thirteen tons a day.

The inefficiency represented by these figures challenged the attention of James Watt, a mathematical instrument maker of the University of Glasgow. From his knowledge of latent heat, a subject recently investigated by Dr. Black of the university, he concluded that five-sixths of the energy of the steam was lost through the fact that the cylinder was alternately heated and cooled to condense the steam. After many years of experiment, during which he received financial assistance from Matthew Boulton, a hardware manufacturer who was faced by the inadequacy of the water power of the little brook on which his Soho plant depended, Watt succeeded in constructing a new type of steam engine, which, as perfected, contained all the principles of the expansion steam engine of today.

The Newcomen engines and the first Watt engines were attached to pumps and no one had as yet mastered the problem of converting the straight line motion of the piston into a circular motion which would permit the use of a steam engine as a prime motive force in industry. In 1782, seven years after the first Watt engine had been installed at Soho, Watt worked out the principles of " circular and parallel motion," and within a few years steam began to replace water power to drive the new cotton spinning and other machines. By 1800, 289 Watt engines of 4543 horse power were in use, and after 1801 their extension was very rapid. France, by way of contrast, is said to have had only 15 engines with a total of about 230 horse power in 1815.

The problem of increasing output might be met in other ways than through the use of machinery or mechanical power to replace human energy. In certain industries, such as pin-making, there was a subdivision of labor among many workers who worked together in one shop under supervision, each performing some small, easily mastered operation. The gain in output made possible by coördinated effort was very striking; and when the essential principles of the subdivision of processes in association with disciplinary supervision were combined with machinery and mechanical power, the modern factory was created.

The credit for the introduction of this new type of productive unit must be divided between Richard Arkwright and John Wilkinson. The first, originally a barber and hair merchant, seems to have appropriated the invention of the water frame, which he patented in 1769 and set up in a small mill, driven by horse power, at Nottingham. He successfully solved the problem of securing operatives who would submit to his discipline by going to the parish workhouses or poorhouses, and apprenticing the children who were inmates of them. In 1785 he installed a steam engine in one of his mills, of which he now had a considerable number; and with this development the main lines of the modern factory were laid down.

In the use of steam in the new industry Arkwright had been preceded by John Wilkinson, the greatest ironmaster of his time. Wilkinson's cannon boring machine made it possible for Watt to bore a true cylinder for his first steam engine, and after that had been completed, the second Watt engine was purchased by Wilkinson to drive his pumps. Some years later, when the principles of circular motion had been worked out, Wilkinson bought a second engine to drive some heavy iron-rolling machines. Although a number of engines were presently in use in rolling mills, it was in the cotton spinning factory that steam received its most rapid and significant extension.

The factory worked by steam power is the most characteristic type of productive unit of the Industrial Revolution, but it must always be kept in mind that its first conquests were limited to such fields as cotton spinning and iron manufacture, and that the domestic system survived until a very late date in nearly all other lines of production. Not until after the Napoleonic wars was the new system extended even to weaving cotton cloth, and in the chain-making trades it was just beginning to be introduced before the Great War in 1914.

For the construction of the new apparatus of transportation and industry, such as the viaducts of the canals, the tires of wagons and stage coaches, and the gears and moving parts of the new machines, iron had the necessary qualifications of strength and lightness, and it was easily worked. Yet in the form in which it was produced in England in the earlier eighteenth century, malleable iron smelted with charcoal, it was limited in quantity on account of the exhaustion of the forests and was also extremely expensive. Experiments had long been under way to replace charcoal with coal, and after three generations of effort the

Darbys of Coalbrookdale succeeded with the help of larger furnaces and increased blasts in using coke as a fuel. The resultant product was not pure malleable or wrought iron of the medieval type, collected in a semi-soft mass at the bottom of the furnaces, but liquid iron of a higher carbon content which, cast in sows and pigs as it left the furnace, came to be called pig iron. Whereas the older types of furnace turned out from five to six tons of iron a week, in 1760 the Coalbrookdale furnaces yielded forty tons a week.

While the new pig iron was suited to many structural purposes, it was too brittle for others because of its high carbon content. Eventually in 1783 two men, Henry Cort and Peter Onions, discovered the process of puddling, by which carbon could be burnt out of the pig iron and a material very similar to the old fashioned malleable iron produced. Puddled iron became the characteristic structural material of industry, and was only replaced by a more modern material, Bessemer steel, after the middle of the nineteenth century.

LARGE SCALE CAPITAL AND IRON MASTERS OF MEN

The whole trend of developments in industry as a result of the increased demands for goods was toward larger scale production. This is, of course, apparent in lines of trade where the factory was introduced, but it was no less true where the domestic system was merely extended and enlarged. In consequence, great capital was required to engage in industry. The factory obviously required heavy investments for the building, machinery, and steam engine; but even where the factory was not yet a feature, the wages of large numbers of domestic workers and heavy stocks of materials, which had constantly to be kept on hand, absorbed money in amounts unusual in industry in earlier times. The contrast between the earlier and later situation is well illustrated by the comparison between the £200 (£91 19s. 3½d. in tools and the rest in cash) with which James Watt and John Craig set up in partnership in 1750 and the £20,000 which Matthew Boulton laid out some years later in building his new works at Soho.

The origin of the new industrial capital is a matter of some interest. It was seldom advanced by the banks, such as the Bank of England, since their business was with commerce, not industry. Occasionally, warehousemen of London, faced by heavier orders than they could fill, advanced to tried and experienced manufacturers the whole cost of a new and larger plant. Bequests and marriage portions sometimes found their way into industry also, but the chief source of the new capital was profits which were returned into industry by the new entrepreneurs, who stinted themselves to the limit, worked like slaves, and lived like slave masters. Starting with £20, derived from a legacy, Josiah Wedgwood, for example, constantly put back his earnings into his pottery works and left them so extensive that they are still one of the largest businesses of the modern world.

The building up of their capital was a consciously recognized duty on the part of the great manufacturers; to their minds the greatest vice was consumption of capital or failure to put it to work in industry. In all this they had no sense of social obligation; their great plants were their own, as they were not slow to assert; and they were making fortunes for themselves and flattered their pride by the size of these fortunes. But although their great fortunes were their own to manage and to enlarge, they were not theirs to waste or consume. Thus in spite of themselves they acted as social trustees who took charge of the social surplus and used it to the full extent of their ability to perfect the industrial plant. Attempts have been made to account for the extraordinary interest in amassing capital and accumulating wealth by the entrepreneurs of this period by reference to the fact that many among them were Quakers, Presbyterians, and other varieties of Dissenters who were permeated with the teaching of John Calvin on the virtue of acquiring wealth. The prevalence of Dissenters among the outstanding manufacturers is very notable, and gives much color of truth to this general point of view.

In spite of the necessity of large investments in the new industry, it is significant that very few who brought large capital sums into manufacturing made much progress, and that those most successful began with little or nothing. "The men who did establish themselves were raised by their own efforts, commencing in a very humble way and pushing their advance by a series of unceasing exertions, having a very limited capital to begin with or none at all save that of their own labor." Sprung from the ranks of mere operatives, small masters, or yeomen, they rose by their quickness of view, energy of character, and large endowment of sagacity.

Theirs was a many-sided job. They had to buy their raw materials and manufacture their goods, and generally, after 1800, they marketed their products in the face of the fiercest competition; they had to devise and administer codes of factory discipline, "the Herculean task" and "noble achievement" of Richard Arkwright; they had to find their labor forces and watch them starve in the midst of a slump. They had to be "Iron Masters of Men," and demanded plenty of elbow room in their conscious task of building up Great Britain's industrial supremacy.

Unfortunately, the earliest manufacturers were men of very limited general information, who saw and knew little of anything beyond the demand for their twist or their cloth and the speediest and best modes for their production. The sprinkling of men of more refined habits among them was extremely scanty. They were thus led to interpret the *desiderata* of policy solely in accord with their own requirements and limited point of view, holding that in the long run their own good and the good of all were identical. As their wealth and influence grew, they succeeded in finding philosophers to work out rational justifications for their attitude, in the doctrine of *laissez faire*, and through their central organization, the Chamber of Manufacturers, they demanded and received from the government such changes in the laws and state policy as they conceived to be in their interests.

In 1785 the organized industrialists objected to a commercial treaty which the government was negotiating with Ireland because they feared the force of Irish competition under the free trade clauses of the agreement, and they succeeded in having certain amendments proposed which the Irish refused to accept. In 1786, finding that, in consequence of the very rapid extension of production facilities, their output had not only caught up with the demand of their existing markets but was outstripping it, they persuaded the government to negotiate the Eden Treaty with France. Under the terms of this document, England was opened to French wines, and French tariffs against English manufactured goods were lowered to the point where English manufacturers in certain lines could compete successfully for the French market.

Later, when the workers began to discover the baneful effects of trade fluctuation, of too rapid expansion and subsequent depression, and the evil consequences of excessive competition among workers for jobs, the workers sought to revive certain sixteenth century laws which would have made it impossible to draw more than a certain number of new workers into an industry within a given time, and which provided means for fixing wages. By this time the thinking of the manufacturing classes had so permeated the minds of the governing classes that the reply of the government to three separate attempts of workingmen to revive the obsolescent Elizabethan labor code was to repeal it in its entirety in 1813–1814. " The true principles of commerce appeared at this time (in the age of Elizabeth) to be misunderstood, and the act in question proved the truth of this assertion. The persons most competent to form regulations with respect to trade were the master manufacturers, whose interest it was to have goods of the best fabric, and no legislative enactment could ever effect so much in producing that result as the merely leaving things to their own courses and operation."

THE NEW INDUSTRY AND THE WORKING CLASSES

The first reactions of the industrial changes of the second half of the eighteenth century were to better the lot of the employed. In the earliest days of factory industry, for example, wherever machinery was used on a large scale, there was a shortage of labor. Wages were high, and the standard of economic well-being was so superior that moralists could protest about the extravagance of the " poor " who " indulge upon many occasions with the wheaten loaf." Wedgwood boasted that the new pottery factories had turned a poverty stricken region into a populous and prosperous district, " with the workmen earning near double their former wages, their houses mostly new and comfortable, and the lands, roads, and every other circumstance bearing evident marks of the most pleasing and rapid improvements."

Unfortunately for the industrial operatives, there was in England one extremely large social class, that of the agricultural laborers, which had upon it the blight of centuries of servility, and was at the moment in process of being degraded still further. As a result of the changes in agriculture, the laborer in the country was being deprived of even the tiniest scrap of land, and was becoming completely dependent upon a money wage, which the farmers were not slow to beat down to the lowest minimum. What this minimum was may be gleaned from some of the model budgets drawn up by such influential men as Arthur Young in 1770, in which the consumption of tea was regarded as a crime; beef, mutton, wheaten bread, and butter were classified as unnecessary luxuries; and the staple diet was reduced to potatoes and rice.

With this class of the agricultural laborer, and with the still more degraded " wild Irish," the factory worker was thrown into competition, as to an even greater extent recruits were brought into the factory towns and villages from the country districts and from Ireland. To maintain his standards in the face of wage reductions, the factory worker consciously married early, begot a large family, and sent his children into the mills so that their pitiful pay might be used to eke out his own earnings. In the end he only added to the severity of the competition and the wretchedness which ensued. The competition of workers with each other for jobs beat down living standards to those of the worst conditioned, and the slight gains made by the first adventurers were overwhelmed and swept away.

To make the lot of the toilers worse came the ugliness of the factory towns, " not the refuge of a civilization, but the barracks of industry "; the crowded, unsanitary houses in which they had to live because they could afford nothing better; the disappearance of " the green grass and the healthful hayfield " as every open space was crowded with houses and factories; and the awful monotony of factory routine. " The whistling of the birds is not for us; our melody is the deafening noise of the engine." " Whilst the engine runs people must work; men, women, and children are yoked together with iron and steam. The animal machine is chained fast to the iron machine which knows no suffering and no weariness."

Since so many of the workers were fresh from the soil, ignorant, cut off from the traditional social restraints and the healthy out-door sports and occupations of their country environment, and unfettered by any sense of civic attachment, it was not unnatural that they should add to their wretchedness by drunkenness and sexual excesses. Where else but in the public house was there escape from the tedium of fourteen hours of tending a machine? Nor is it remarkable that three-fourths of the girls and women of factory towns were said to be unchaste.

" THE FLUCTUATING BASIS OF TRADE "

As long as society was contained in isolated areas, in which each group lived its own life, a local crop failure might bring famine but it was scarcely felt outside the limits of the district. But as soon as Europe became more closely united, through the development of physical means of transportation and of the less palpable bonds of business connections, every major fluctuation was felt through the whole organism. Both the manufacturer and his hands were at the mercy of a change in fashions in Vienna, the failure of a banking house in Edinburgh or Amsterdam, a revolt in India, too rapid expansion in the production of everything from pottery clay to tea, and, above all, of war in Europe. Beginning in 1763 these crises grew in scope with each decade; and, after the beginning of the Revolutionary wars with France, they developed extraordinary intensity. To meet orders for war materials after 1793 industry was developed very rapidly; more and more laborers were drafted, more capital enlisted, and high profits and good wages prevailed. But a year or two afterwards the end of a coalition, the acceptance of a truce, or the arrangement of a treaty would withdraw the forces of one country or another from the field, there would be a drop in orders, works would shut down and operatives would be thrown out of employment.

The manufacturing classes had hitherto been indifferent to politics; they would wear no " party-colored robe." This old tradition, together with the fear of political change engendered in all the propertied classes by the Revolutionary movement in France, kept them from demanding political reform now, and it was not until after 1815 that they identified themselves with that cause.

The industrial workers who found themselves without work while food prices mounted ever higher as the result of poor crops and currency inflation followed two lines of agitation. In London, they demanded political reform and were harried into secrecy and treasonable practices for their presumption. In the north of England, where the factories were beginning to dot the land, the workers banded into unions for collective bargaining with their employers. Their economic unions caused as much apprehension as the political clubs, and just at the end of the century they, too, were declared illegal by statute. But neither the political club nor the trade union could be forgotten; and workingmen of all countries, whenever they were disgruntled, resorted to one or the other.

CHAPTER II

THE AGE OF COAL AND IRON

IMPORTANT as the social and economic developments in England in the latter part of the eighteenth century were, they were only a faint foreshadowing of the vastly greater changes of the half century or so after 1815 or 1820. Certain phenomena continued in an intensified form. Among these was the most rapid rate of increase in the population of which the historian has any knowledge. France added to her people by 20 per cent between 1820 and 1870; Germany, 55 per cent; and England, 83 per cent. Of almost equal significance was the growing urbanization of life. The population of the country districts continued to grow, but its rate of augmentation was very small in comparison with the figures for the nations as a whole. The overwhelming gains were made by the cities. In France, for example, Paris doubled in size between 1801 and 1850, and Lyons a little more than doubled. In England, in a single decade, from 1821 to 1831, Sheffield, Birmingham, Manchester, Liverpool, Leeds, and Bradford all gained more than 40 per cent, while London had already well under way that extraordinary development which was to give her, before the end of the century, a greater population than Holland, Sweden, or Portugal. The census of 1851 showed that in Great Britain, for the first time in any large country in the world's history, one-half of the people lived in cities. Since under modern conditions the rate and character of the growth of towns is the best indication of the extent of the industrialization of life, these figures are symptomatic of unprecedented progress in that direction.

At the basis of this growth in numbers and this shift from the country to the town was a complex of many forces. Advances in medical science and surgery continued apace, culminating in the work of Pasteur, who discovered the significance of microbes and germs in causing disease, of Lister, who laid the foundations of antiseptic surgery, and of Koch, whose discovery that bacteria could be grown outside the human body has led to the more recent development of toxins and antitoxins. The exploitation of the colonial world still continued its effects as in the former period. Probably of greater importance was a new speed of living in town and country, a new willingness to work harder and to produce more on the part of the farmer, the miner, and the manufacturer.

The stimulus to greater effort and the promise of larger rewards were given by the closer proximity between places created by improvements in communication and transport. Time and space in distance were sharply lessened; districts recently remote were brought psychologically and physically closer to each other. Farmers found themselves enjoying easy access to markets where they could exchange their produce for an increasing variety of manufactured goods, into the creation of which labor and coal, cotton and iron, and the other basic supplies of nineteenth century life entered. The area from which supplies could be effectively drawn was enormously widened and the distribution of finished goods in exchange similarly extended. This development involved, naturally enough, areas within the same country, but it strode over national frontiers and even brought distant continents within closer touch. In 1850 New York was only a little further from London than Liverpool had been in 1750, and Paris was closer than Canterbury had been.

THE COMING OF THE RAILROAD AND THE TELEGRAPH

The first element in the extraordinary development in the means of communication postulated in this generalization consisted in the continuation of the road and canal building of the eighteenth century. By 1830 England had approximately 20,000 miles of turnpike roads, over which thousands of coaches ran each day at speeds which reached the maximum of ten miles an hour on the four hundred mile journey from London to Edinburgh. There were also 4670 miles of canals and improved rivers, and so heavy was the freight traffic over these that in 1824 the Trent and Mersey Company paid 75 per cent in dividends, the Coventry Canal, 44 per cent, and the Loughborough Canal, 175 per cent.

In France the Restoration government at once set about to repair the great main highways, two-thirds of which had been left in bad condition at the end of the Napoleonic wars. It also embarked upon a regular program of canal construction which by 1848 added 2900 kilometres of navigations to the 1200 previously in existence. The Rhine was joined to the Rhone, the Marne to the Rhine, and the Aisne to the Marne, by some of the more important canal projects of this period; and the great activity of the Second Empire and Third Republic lay in modernizing and standardizing the system rather than in extending it.

In Germany progress was slower. Prussia had only about 2000 (English) miles of road all told in 1816, all but 800 miles in her western provinces. It was not until 1845 that Prussia began her greatest activity, but between that time and 1870 she completed her modern road system. The complicated political boundaries in Germany before 1870 rather retarded German canal construction until after the beginning of the empire.

Before the road and canal systems of Europe were actually completed, they were overwhelmed by the railroad, the most pregnant invention of the nineteenth century. Tram roads or dram roads were already well known in England before 1800. As early as Charles I's reign, Master Beaumont built a dram road of wooden rails at Newcastle, and in the eighteenth century roads with rails were extensively used in connection with collieries and as feeders to canals. The rail was now covered with iron — in some cases cast iron plate-rails with flanges to keep the wheels of the wagons in place were used; in others, edge rails, upon which wagons were kept in position by flanges on their own tires. So extensive was the use of these tramways that Wales contained 150 miles of lines before 1815, one of them over twenty miles in length. In the region of Newcastle there were 225 miles of iron roads, and there were considerable stretches in the Forest of Dean. In 1801 a railroad for general traffic open to the public was built from Wandsworth to Croydon, outside London.

On all these lines wagons were drawn by horses, although as early as 1804 Richard Trevithick had placed a locomotive on rails in Wales. In 1821 Thomas Gray published his *Observations on a General Iron Railway or Land Steam Conveyance; to supersede the Necessity of Horses in all Public Vehicles,* which argued for the general adoption of the locomotive engine; and already George Stephenson was conducting his experiments, although when William James argued with him that speeds of twenty or thirty miles an hour might be attained, Stephenson refused to think of more than eight or ten. William Huskisson, President of the Board of Trade, considered even ten miles an hour so horrible that in a speech in the House of Commons he predicted that the smoke and noise, the hiss and roar of locomotive engines passing at ten or twelve miles an hour would bring dismay even to the cattle plowing in the field or grazing in the meadows.

When, in the early twenties, a line with wooden rails was projected from Stockton to Darlington to tap the South Durham coal field, Stephenson persuaded the directors to use a steam engine and iron rails, which had recently been brought to a considerable state of perfection. Stephenson's first engine (1825), which had a maximum speed of eight miles an hour, and whose chimney got red hot as soon as any speed was attained, was so costly to run that the use of steam was almost abandoned by the Stockton and Darlington Company, when Hackworth designed the *Royal George* locomotive which was cheaper than horses. Four years later, 1829, when the Manchester and Liverpool Railroad was nearing completion, a competition was held to determine the character of the motive power. Stephenson entered his *Rocket* locomotive, and when the road opened in 1830 the *Rocket* drew the first train. William Huskisson, stepping out on the track to see whether the train was coming, was struck by it; and, as he was being rushed to receive medical attention, the *Rocket* made almost thirty miles an hour.

Coaches drawn by horses were run on the first lines in the intervals between the steam-drawn trains, but by 1835 the superiority of the locomotive was so well established that nothing more was heard of horses.

The decade after 1830 witnessed the building of many short stretches of important lines, and by 1840 nearly eight hundred miles of railroad had been built in England. Then in 1844 projection and construction began with a rush. A veritable railroad mania swept the country; by 1850 over six thousand miles were built in Great Britain and, by 1870, fifteen thousand miles.

The advantages of the new system of transportation, which cut down the time of travel to one-fifth of that of the fastest stage coaches, were early recognized in other countries. France and Belgium both had some tramway lines as early as the eighteenth century, and in the eighteen twenties there was in France a good deal of construction of horse-worked railway. In 1826 an experimental line was laid down at Elberfeld in Germany; but it was the success of the *Rocket* on the Manchester and Liverpool road that aroused real excitement. France got her first locomotive in 1832; in 1833 Friedrich List published his pamphlet, *Of a Saxon railway system as foundation for a general German system,* in which he foresaw the main German system as it was afterward built; and in 1835, in spite of the warnings of the Bavarian College of Physicians that traveling in trains would cause horrible headaches, the first German line, five miles long, was built from Nuremberg to Fürth in Bavaria. The first Belgian line, from Brussels to Malines, was opened in the same year.

By 1850 it was possible to travel from the North Sea to the Adriatic on the German-Austrian lines, " the most remarkable piece of continuous railway in Europe," and the French main lines were nearly completed. The next decades were given over chiefly to building the subsidiary network and in amplifying the facilities of the main lines.

In the railroad construction of Europe all countries made rapid progress, but scarcely two countries followed the same policy. In Great Britain private enterprise took the initiative and provided all the costs, subject to a charter from Parliament, which only sought to maintain competition. In Belgium a program of state construction was adopted at the outset and until 1850 all lines were state constructed and state owned; but between 1850 and 1870 the new construction, nearly three times that previously carried out, was in private hands. In France almost a decade of debate preceded the adoption of the national railway program, and when a decision was reached in 1842, it was not completely carried out. In a general way, in France, the state coöperated with private capital in construction, with the reserved right of ownership to the state; it controlled the geographical plan of the various systems; and it exercised effective supervision over rates, safety devices, conditions of travel, and so forth. Hanover and other German states built their own lines. Prussia exercised the strictest control over construction, which was carried through by private capital, but after 1879 it began the purchase of the private lines and virtually the whole Prussian system became the property of the state. Only a very few unimportant stretches continued to remain in private ownership.

Concurrently with the railroad construction a network of telegraph wires spread over Europe, to bring people into still more immediate touch, and to make of Europe, and then the world, a single market. Experiments with carrying messages by electricity had been under way in Germany and in the United States in the thirties, and in 1836 success was achieved in both countries; but the system of S. F. Morse, the American, was the one universally adopted. In 1843 the first electric telegraph line in England was opened between Paddington and Slough; in 1851 a submarine cable was laid between England and France; and in 1866, after several earlier attempts had failed, Cyrus Field laid the first transatlantic cable.

OCEAN SHIPPING

What the railroad did for Europe, and for America too, the sailing ship and the steamship did for intercontinental communication. Steam had less importance on the sea in the period which ended in 1870 or so than on the land, since the ocean steamship was still really in the experimental stage until the middle seventies. The sailing ship was the ocean carrier *par excellence* of the age and reached a remarkable state of perfection. At the same time it must always be kept in mind that the sailing ship did not work a transformation commensurate with that of the railroad. Although the sailers were fast, it was still a hundred days from England to China; the ships themselves continued comparatively small, and the total tonnage was limited.

Although British ships unquestionably dominated the seas in 1815, they represented no advance in design for many a generation. There were few ships above 500 tons burden, except the money-eating 1500 ton East Indiamen of the British East India Company, and all were slow, and inefficient. The first improvements came with the American West India free-traders, blockade runners in the period of the Napoleonic wars; the Baltimore brigs; and the 450 ton Medford East Indiamen, which with a crew of 18 men carried one-half the cargo of the 1500 ton British East Indiaman with its complement of 150 men. American skill reached its culmination in the great clipper ships of the period 1850–1855, such as the 2421 ton *Sovereign of the Seas,* the largest of the clippers, the *Lightning,* which sailed

436 nautical miles in twenty-four hours (18 to 18½ knots per hour), and the *James Baines,* which made the voyage from Boston to Liverpool in twelve days and six hours in 1854. The British soon copied the American lines, and presently (after 1850) built clippers of their own of teak wood and iron, rather than of the " soft " wood of which the American vessels were constructed. The hundred days' races of such clippers as the *Ariel* and the *Taeping* home from China with the new season's tea were sporting events for twenty years.

Until as late as 1860 the sailing ships held their own, not only in the amount of absolute tonnage afloat, but in the amount of annual construction. In 1870 sailing tonnage was still in the lead, but the new construction of the past decade had been chiefly steamships. Yet it was not until twenty years later that steamers dominated the seas, and that sailing tonnage declined to a position of minor importance.

The invention of the steamship is generally attributed to Robert Fulton of New York in 1807, although it must be remembered that he had predecessors, such as Robert Fitch, and that contemporaries, such as Henry Bell, were at work on the same problem in Europe. Within a generation or so after 1807 small steamers were to be found on many European rivers, in the coasting trade (in summer) and in the cross-channel and North Sea services. As early as 1819 the *Savannah* had used steam as an auxiliary power to cross the Atlantic, and in 1838 four steamships made the transatlantic voyage, although the only one to remain in regular service continued to lose money for her owners.

Until wood was replaced by iron in the hulls to give more cargo space for the same weight of hull, a process which began in the 1830's, but was not established until the 1860's, until the paddle wheel was supplanted by the propeller after 1870, and until the engines were so improved that the major portion of the cargo space was not occupied by coal, a step which was made possible by the invention of the compound expansion engine in the 1850's and its universal use after 1870, the steamship was still impracticable for the world's commerce.

When comparative perfection was attained, Great Britain held the lead. Compared with Great Britain's 1,113,000 tons of steam shipping in 1870, France with 154,000 tons of steam shipping, Holland with 19,000 tons, Norway with 14,000 tons, and Germany with 82,-000 tons were hopelessly out of the running; and the competition of the United States had been ended by British-built commerce destroyers during the Civil War.

By bringing the producer and consumer more closely together, and by extending the effective area from which supplies could be drawn and over which products could be sold, the improved sailing ship and the steamship, the telegraph, and, above all, the railroad quickened demand and production to an unprecedented degree. But apart from their contributory effect upon nineteenth century life, these new agencies themselves were enormous consumers of material goods, the demand for which was one of the major stimuli to nineteenth century business. The construction of the physical property of the railroads of Europe, for example, required such quantities of materials as had never entered into men's imaginations, and every market into which the railroad entered as a purchaser, whether for steel rails, for upholstery for its carriages, for machinery for its locomotives, or for coal to run its trains, was stirred into vigorous life. In 1841 the weight of iron in rails and chairs used for a single mile of track was 156 tons; and on this basis the new construction of the year 1847–8 in Great Britain alone required 400,000 tons of iron, without any allowances for bridges, stations, or rolling stock. Treitschke declared that the railroads changed the whole face of the land and "first dragged the nation from its economic stagnation," and Disraeli attributed to the construction of the railroads the whole causation for the prosperity of mid-Victorian England.

AGRICULTURAL PROGRESS

If adequate statistics were available, as they are not, it would probably be possible to show how with every building of a road, canal, or especially a railway line, the farming in the district which it tapped was galvanized into new activity. While the course of this progress cannot be mapped in this concrete way, it is possible to say something about its general nature. Everywhere in western Europe the events of the later eighteenth century and of the French Revolution had either swept away, or prepared for the disappearance of, medieval field systems, and personal serfdom and subjection, although it was not until after 1850 that the work was complete in Germany. With the abolition of restrictive communal control over the land and the consolidation of the holdings, agricultural progress was possible, but many factors, such as subservience to tradition, reluctance to accept changes, and plain ignorance, conditioned the rapidity of improvements.

The lead was taken by England, where notable advances had already been made in the eighteenth century, and where the reaction between growing population and increased supplies was already well established. Politico-legal burdens, such as the poor rates and the tithes, were lightened by the new Poor Law of 1834 and the conversion of tithes into money payments in 1836. Much attention was paid to drainage, one of the most serious problems of English agriculture, and a real solution was found with the invention of the cylindrical drainage tile in 1843, and of a machine to manufacture it cheaply in 1845. In 1840 and 1842 Justus von Liebig issued from his laboratory at Giessen his two epoch making books on agricultural chemistry, on the basis of which artificial manures came into common use in the next decades, stimulated in England by the research work of the agricultural institute at Rothamsted. Steam was used for cultivating just after the middle of the century, and applied to plowing a few years later. So remarkable was the gain in production, that although England was importing greater quantities of grain from Prussia and the Baltic with each year because of the extremely rapid rise of her population, she was feeding over five million more people on her own wheat in 1849 than in 1811.

In France the first real advance was the reduction of the amount of fallow, since as late as 1815 one-half

the land in the south and one-third the land in the north
lay idle each year. This was accomplished in part
through the gradual popularization of the potato, which
had been advocated in the reign of Louis XVI but re-
jected by the peasants and even, as late as the Napoleonic era, considered good enough only for beasts, *les
malheureux*, hungry mountaineers, and the proletariat
of Lyons. Turnip cultivation, so successful in England, made slow progress, but more was done with the
sugar beet, and with artificial meadows, clover, sain-
foin, and lucerne in coördination with a crop rotation
copied from Flanders.

Improvements were also made in stock. The royal
stud farm founded at Rambouillet in 1786 began to
produce results at the time of the Restoration, and the
improved breeds were spread by the larger landowners.
Lafayette popularized the merino sheep between 1801
and 1830; in 1825 the Durham shorthorns were introduced from England; and experiments began at about
this time to improve the native French breeds, such as
the Percheron horses.

One of the most curious things about French agriculture in this period is that what progress was made
was almost entirely achieved without the help of modern
farm machinery. Up to 1860 only a very small percentage of farms had any heavy implements except a
plow. It was only during the next thirty years that
machinery was more generally adopted, and it did not
become universal until the period 1892–1914. The
continuance of patient hand labor made possible that
artistic touch necessary to luxury produce, such as

mushrooms, asparagus, flowers, and strawberries, specialization in which was made profitable by the improvements in transport. After 1846 the good things to eat of French origin were to be found everywhere in Europe.

The agricultural progress of France, notable as it was, was outdistanced across the Rhine. Under the leadership of the junkers, who resembled the English squires in their traditions of service to their families and the state, and who, moreover, did not rent their estates to farmers, but generally kept them in hand and worked hard at their cultivation, the manors of eastern Germany became the models of farming in Europe. England was consciously imitated in such matters as implements, improved stock, and better rotation of crops with clover or grasses on the fallow and roots as a field crop; but to the English example were added close attention to bookkeeping, the popularization of agricultural information by cattle shows, exhibitions of implements, agricultural societies, and agricultural courses and colleges, and finally the study of agricultural chemistry initiated by Justus von Liebig.

The rapid acceptance of new agricultural practices in Germany was in part due to the beet sugar industry, which was well established by 1845. For the best results the sugar beet demanded the most careful cultivation; deep plowing, proper rotation of crops and intensive application of fertilizer to renew the soil, the development of a beet which would give the maximum yield of sugar, and the use of the pulp as cattle fodder brought even the smaller cultivators to appreciate the value of science and its application in farming. The

potato also stimulated agriculture. Not only did it
make good Prussians, as Frederick the Great realized in
the eighteenth century, but it provided cheap fodder
and helped to maintain the numbers of cattle necessary to good agriculture. So remarkable were the effects of the improved methods that, in spite of the very
rapid growth in population, Germany continued to be
self-supporting until the decade 1870–1880, and even
after that produced a very large part of her own food
requirements.

COTTON AND WOOL

As in the eighteenth century the colonial world continued to supply Europe with some of the basic materials for her life, but the emphasis was shifted in the
middle quarter of the nineteenth century from sugar
and similar articles to cotton and wool. Cotton was not
grown in western Europe at all, and the tremendous
cotton textile development would have been impossible
without increasing supplies first from the United States,
upon which all Europe was dependent until the beginning of the American Civil War, and later from Egypt.
Wool was, of course, produced in every country in Europe in great quantities all through the nineteenth century; but the sheep was the one farm animal which
diminished rapidly in numbers as the century advanced.
In France, for example, sheep declined from thirty-two
million head in 1840 to sixteen million in 1911, and in
Germany from twenty-five million in 1873 to five million in 1912. South Africa, Australia, and New Zealand were raising cheaper, if not better, meat and

fleeces, which added to the food of the city proletariats and provided them with one of the staples for their industry.

No discussion of the increase in the basic supplies of nineteenth century life would be complete which omitted the exploitation of the earth's resources in coal and iron ore. These were so vital to the civilization of the time that a recent historian has pointed out that Bismarck's boast that the German Empire was founded on " blood and iron " would be more accurate if rendered " coal and iron." It was the railroads which first demanded large supplies of coal and iron, and the railroads acted as both carriers and consumers in bringing the raw material from the mines and buying the product.

The progress of iron ore production is difficult to describe in itself because of the varying iron content of the ore; some indication of the process will be found in the discussion of the production of pig iron and steel. The story of coal is more easily portrayed. In 1816 Great Britain was perhaps raising 16,000,000 tons of coal. The South Durham coal field was hardly touched and the value of the South Welsh field for steam coal was unrealized. On the continent the Belgian collieries were developing rapidly in the Mons country. France, where the coal measures were remote and inaccessible, lagged behind, although there had been coal workings at Anzin, Alais, and Carmaux in the eighteenth century. For a long time France was producing less than

Belgium, but she could show a rise of from 800,000 tons in 1815 to 5,153,000 in 1847. Further east, the Ruhr and Roer fields were just beginning to be worked in 1815; the Silesian field was untouched until 1840; and in 1846 Prussia took from the Saar, the Ruhr, the Roer, and Silesia only 3,200,000 tons.

With the spread of the railroad, production was more rapid. Great Britain remained in the lead, with a production which mounted to 118,000,000 tons in 1870. Far behind her were Germany with 37,000,000 tons of coal and lignite in 1871, France with 13,000,000 tons of coal, and Belgium with 13,000,000 tons. The total production, which was to rise with extreme rapidity in the next period, represents one of the most significant augmentations in essential materials in the nineteenth century.

NINETEENTH CENTURY INDUSTRIAL DEVELOPMENTS

The greater activity of more people, all working as producers in one field or another, created enormous demands for supplies and products from these same people in their capacity as consumers. The satisfaction of the rising demand for food has already been indicated in the general discussion of agricultural progress; in industry supply was kept abreast of demand by a remarkable series of technical improvements in manufacturing processes, and by fundamental changes in types of industrial organization.

In a general way the technical changes involved the more complete supplanting of human skill by ingenious mechanism, and a very rapid increase in the rate of op-

eration of the machinery, both of which processes made
inevitable the use of steam power. Inventions were
directed further toward the use of cheaper materials or
of smaller quantities of materials for the same amount
of product by the elimination of waste. To meet new
industrial requirements new varieties of product and
even new products might be created. Changes in industrial organization swept away the domestic work-
shop in favor of the factory, and this tended to become
a larger and larger unit as time advanced. The individual entrepreneur working with his own capital was
replaced by the partnership, and this in turn by the
joint stock company, in which the business was directed
by a salaried technical expert, and the capital was provided by men who had no knowledge of the business
in which they invested. Everywhere the largest operations were on such a scale that even the soundest companies could not finance them with their own resources,
and credit provided by great banks, which moblized the
capital resources of a nation or a district, became a vital
part of the industrial process.

Most characteristic of the technical advances of the
period are those in the cotton and iron trades. In spite
of all that had been done with machinery in the eighteenth century, cotton spinning still demanded much
skilled labor in 1820, and the increase in the number of
mules led the spinners to take advantage of the situation to demand higher wages. Attempts were therefore
made to make the mule entirely automatic, and in
1825–30 Messrs. Sharp and Roberts of Manchester
patented and perfected a self-acting or automatic mule,

which dispensed with skilled labor and turned out stronger and more uniform yarn. In the years which followed the mule was constantly enlarged. Whereas an average mule had 300 to 350 spindles in 1836, the mule of 1886 averaged 750 spindles and might have 1200. Spindles were, moreover, revolved more rapidly; in 1819–21 a spindle produced two hanks of 40 yarn a day; in 1882, four hanks.

In the weaving trades, nearly all work was by hand until 1822, even though Edmund Cartwright had evolved the principles of the power loom in the period after 1784. It was not until the power loom was improved and refined that wide use was possible, but between 1822 and 1833 from 90,000 to 100,000 power looms were built. In the same period the number of hand looms increased from 240,000 to 250,000. In 1841 Messrs. Kenworthy and Bullough produced an automatic power loom, which soon drove the hand loom weaver to wage a losing fight with starvation. The power loom of 1836 had a speed of from 90 to 112 picks (throws of the shuttle) a minute; in 1875 the number was 170 to 200 a minute, and in the middle 1880's looms were built to make 400 picks a minute. In 1840 a man and a boy could operate two looms; in 1880 one man could supervise from four to six looms.

The characteristic metal of the late eighteenth and early nineteenth century was puddled iron, the manufacture of which has already been described. It suited all requirements in the period before 1855, and the great effort of the ironmasters was to produce it more quickly, more cheaply, and from the more abundant ores. The first success was achieved in 1828, when J. B. Neilson heated the blast in the Carron works in Scotland. The hot blast made possible the smelting of ore with only one-third as much coal as before, and it permitted the use of the blackband ironstone of Scotland, hitherto little smelted.

During the Crimean War Henry Bessemer became interested in an improved projectile, in view of the inefficiency of the French and English guns at Sebastopol. After he had developed the rifled barrel, he found that the existing material of which cannons were made was not strong enough to stand the heavy charges of explosive necessary for the complete success of his idea. He, therefore, set about to produce a new material capable of meeting the strains and stresses to which he wished to subject it. The result was Bessemer steel, a material useful not only for cannon, but for steel rails, soon to become essential in place of iron rails on account of the increase in weight and size of trains.

When it was learned that only certain ores could be worked successfully by the Bessemer process, two chemists, Thomas and Gilchrist, set about to find a method for using the phosphorus-bearing ores, of which there were enormous deposits in Europe, to produce a steel which resembled Bessemer steel. In 1879 they perfected the Thomas-Gilchrist basic process, which gave extraordinary significance to the vast minette deposits which Germany had acquired with Lorraine in 1870. Other technicians were concerned with the problem of a steel equally cheap as the Bessemer steel, but capable of taking different degrees of malleability, ductility, and softness. This problem was solved by the Siemens-Martin open hearth process in 1864–1867.

LARGE SCALE PRODUCTION

As a consequence of growing mechanization, the whole trend of industry was toward the factory and large scale production. Yet care must be taken to guard against the assumption that the factory early became universal, or that large scale production was general at an early date. Even in England where factories were more rapidly introduced than in Europe, they long continued small, and domestic work was not supplanted until late in many lines of trade. The development can be traced in part by the extension of the use of the steam engine, an almost necessary adjunct to the nineteenth century factory, and in part by the study of industrial census reports.

As a basis of comparison with the figures which follow, it may be noted that, in 1907, 10,755,009 horse power was produced in the United Kingdom, of which 1,239,212 horse power of steam and water origin, plus some electric power, was used in the cotton industry. In 1830 cotton factories used 30,000 horse power of steam installation and 10,000 horse power of water installation. In 1850 the figures were 71,000 and 11,000 horse power respectively. Other English textile factories in 1850 used 47,000 horse power, of which 34,000 was steam and 13,000 water. These figures are even more significant when it is noted that the textile branches used most of the power generated in the second quarter of the nineteenth century, and many industries used little or no power in England as late as 1850. In the milling of grain and in the woodworking trades, including the arduous operations of sawing, power was practically absent.

Other figures for England tend also to modify the impression of overwhelming concentration which generalizations about the growth of industrial units sometimes create. In 1851, of 677 firms in the engineering trades, 457 employed less than 10 men, and only 14 employed 350 or more. At the same time there were fewer than a hundred cotton firms in the last category of large businesses employing over 350 men. As late as 1898 the average force of the 8500 power-using factories in London was 41 workers; and, if the 750 largest companies are omitted, the average was only 20 workers.

In France there were traditions of the use of machinery and larger scale industry before 1815. The recent work of a group of French scholars makes it evident that before 1789, while Great Britain was experiencing her first notable industrial expansion, France was in the midst of something of the same kind. While it was possible to meet increased demand in most cases merely by extending the domestic system, English cotton spinning machines began to be introduced in considerable numbers after 1786, and large scale plants were set up for printing calicoes, for silk-throwing, and for metallurgical work at Creusot and Indret.

The opening of French markets to English manufactured goods by the Eden Treaty in 1786 adversely affected certain lines of business and strengthened the hand of the mercantilists, who, coming into political power under the guise of Jacobins after the Revolution, tried to reimpose the protective policy of the eighteenth century. Their work was the basis of Napoleon's more grandiose scheme, involved in the Continental System, to give to French manufactures the markets of the continent through the exclusion and prohibition of English goods. Owing to the shortage of raw materials, such as cotton, the importation of which from overseas was prevented by the British fleet, and perhaps owing to the fact that French manufacturers were so busy on war orders that they could not satisfy the requirements of the normal European markets, Napoleon's project failed, although the output of French industry was increased during the war years from 894 million francs in 1788 to 1747 million francs in 1812.

Important contributions to industrial progress had been made, moreover, by French technicians and scientists. In 1786 Berthollet applied chlorine to bleaching, and the eight months process of hand bleaching of cotton was reduced to two days. In 1801 Joseph Jacquard invented the Jacquard loom for weaving elaborate patterns. Somewhat later Achard of Berlin perfected a process of refining beet sugar, to make good the cutting off of colonial sugar supplies.

Notwithstanding notable achievements, France had undergone none of the transformation which was visible in England in 1815. In all France there were only about fifteen steam engines in 1815, used exclusively for pumping in the mines. By 1830, there were 625 of 10,000 horse power and, by 1848, 5200 engines of 65,000 horse power. English textile mills used more steam power in 1839 than all France in 1848.

In spite of the presence of a few large works, such as Le Creusot with 1200 hands in 1836, the domestic system remained intact in France up to 1850. Vigorous industrial progress began only with the completion of the railway network in 1855–1860, but the rapid expansion, the real industrial revolution in France, did not begin until the 'nineties. Until then the average French power-using factory was very small indeed. Only in the generation 1890–1910 did larger units become significant. As late as 1896 the average number of workers in the 575,000 " industrial establishments " of France was 5.5, and only 151 factories had more than 1000 people, while 400,000 had one or two work people.

The process of industrialization in Germany began later than that of France, but when once it started it went ahead with extraordinary speed. In the Germany of 1840 large enterprises were exceedingly rare, although a little had been done in the eighteenth century by princely patronage to set up occasional factories to print calicoes; and there were important sugar refineries at Hamburg and Bremen. In 1837 Berlin had 390 horse power of steam, and all Prussia, including the Saar and the coal fields of the Rhine and of Silesia, employed only 7500 horse power for all industrial purposes in metallurgy, spinning, and milling. In 1846 there were 22,000 horse power in use, of which 14,000 was in mining and metallurgical establishments.

Industry was almost universally in the hands of *Verleger*, who employed domestic cottage workers, or of small independent masters working with one or two apprentices and journeymen. Iron, for example, was smelted in hundreds of very tiny furnaces owned by artisans who found by-employment on the land. There were already a few larger works; a machine shop in Berlin employing two hundred men, an iron works at Ruhrort where " the order, quiet, and businesslike arrangements were quite English," and " Messrs. Krupp and Company's " works at Essen which produced a very fine grade of cast steel, some of which succeeded in finding a market because it was palmed off as of English origin. The large plants were, however, exceptional; the real German industry was represented by the smallest enterprises.

The acceleration of German industrial development was first conspicuous after about 1845. In the 'fifties the " rush to the cities " began, although this must not be taken too literally, since Prussia was still 67.5 per cent rural in 1870 as compared with 71.5 per cent in 1852 and 73.5 per cent in 1816. For all Germany the 1870 figures for rural population were 63.9 per cent, but in 1910 only 40 per cent lived in the country and 60 per cent of the vastly larger population lived in the cities.

Up to 1860 the progress of industrial change was slow, but in the late 'sixties and early 'seventies things went with a whirl. German pig iron production in 1860 was one-sixth of that of Great Britain and much less than that of France. In 1880 it was one-third of that of Great Britain; in 1900 it almost equaled that of

Great Britain and in 1910 it was 14,794,000 tons, over four million tons more than that of Great Britain. Similar increases in output were to be discovered in Germany's textile and other industries, and in association with these developments there was nearly always the introduction of the modern factory, which tended, as in Great Britain and France, to assume larger proportions in the last decade of the nineteenth century.

The changes in the size of the industrial units were accompanied everywhere by important developments in the form and nature of ownership. The individual or family ownership continued, and is still to be found in some of the greatest of all industrial undertakings, such as the Ford Company in the United States. But partnerships were also very common in the early half of the nineteenth century; and, as the company required more capital for enlargements, it often arranged to allow sleeping partners to make investments. On the continent, under the French Commercial Code of 1807, such sleeping partners had limited liability although the partners did not, and the investments of the sleeping partners might be split up into regular shares, and, after a court decision of 1832 in France permitting the issue of the certificates of sleeping partnership to bearers, the *sociétés en commandite sur actions* became very popular. There was also on the continent the *société anonyme,* the joint stock company, with official sanction and close official supervision. This was used particularly for public utility works and for banking and insurance companies.

In England partnerships were especially important

all through the first half of the nineteenth century because of the traditional dislike of joint stock companies going back to the South Sea Bubble, and because of the legal difficulties of securing a charter for such a company. But owing to the fact that under the common law there was no limit to the liability of sleeping partners for losses suffered in business, and that the law officers of the crown refused to recommend the alteration of the law in 1837, a strong demand arose from industrial leaders in need of capital for fundamental changes in the law. So little foresighted was the royal commission appointed in 1852 to consider the subject that it reported in 1854 against any modification, on the ground that the only cases in addition to railway, dock, and shipping companies (which were able to stand the expense of parliamentary charters) where limited liability was desirable were in the establishment of baths, wash houses, lodging houses, and reading rooms, which could not attract men of great capital. Humble capital might be tempted into such enterprises by limited liability.

In spite of the apparent scorn with which the royal commission viewed such small sums as one or two hundred pounds, the manufacturers wanted the money, and between 1855 and 1862 they forced the English company laws to be subjected to a general revision, which permitted the easy creation of joint stock and limited liability companies. Small amounts of capital could now be mobilized for industrial purposes more completely than before, and the subsequent growth in industry is in no small measure due to this fact.

The importance of the small investor and the value of his capital was realized in Germany in the midst of the great expansion which attended the foundation of the empire. In 1870–1872 a general company law for the empire was passed, with limited liability as an essential feature; but since the elaborate supervision of this law was felt to make it unsuited to smaller or confidential enterprises, it was decided to adopt a second form of company with limited liability, but without masses of marketable shares. The joint stock limited liability company was the *Aktiengesellschaft;* the second and smaller type of company was the *Gesellschaft mit beschränkter Haftung,* G.m.b.H.

The general tendency of industry to organize itself under the various joint stock and limited liability forms is seen in the formation of five hundred companies a year in France in 1896, a thousand in 1899, and over fifteen hundred a year in 1910–1912. In Germany there were 2100 joint stock companies in 1886–7, and 5400 in 1912 with an average capitalization of $800,-000; in 1893 there were 200 associations with limited liability (G.m.b.H.), 9000 in 1907, and 16,500 in 1909, with an average capitalization of $55,000. The United Kingdom in 1909 contained 46,000 companies, with a capital of £3,360,000,000.

On the extended scale on which business operations were being conducted in the latter years of the period under discussion, the regular capitalization of the several varieties of industrial enterprises no longer sufficed for all purposes. Manufacturers had to resort to credit and borrowing, and in response to their requirements the powerful industrial banks, such as the Bank of Liverpool and Martins in England, the Deutsche Bank and the Dresdner Bank in Germany, and the Credit Lyonnais in France came into existence. These industrial banks not merely provided credit for industry, but went further to float securities and even to establish new companies. " In Germany " according to Herr Schuster of the Dresdner Bank, " our banks are largely responsible for the development of the Empire, having fostered and built up its industries. It is from 1871 that our real development dates, and it is since that year our great banks have been organized. . . . To them more than to any other agency may be credited the splendid results so far achieved."

THE INDUSTRIAL WORKERS AND LABOR UNIONISM

One of the most significant results of the introduction of the joint stock company form was that the ownership of industry became an impersonal corporation, the members of which had in large part no knowledge of the business in which they invested their capital. For a limited risk they drew to themselves the profits of a business which was managed and run for them by highly trained and highly paid technical experts, who held their positions only on the condition that they produce maximum dividends. The increasing size of industrial units had long made it apparent that the ordinary workingman no longer had any opportunity of becoming an independent master; the impersonality of the joint stock company rendered impossible those personal touches between master and men which in the earlier days of the factory occasionally robbed such knowledge of its bitterness.

At the same time the workers became conscious of their common interests through association in factories, and through the concentration of labor in the same lines in small geographic areas, as industries developed as a result of natural conditions or sought the same districts because of favorable marketing or transport arrangements. This development came by trades rather than by countries, but in general it was earliest in those nations where the transition to large scale plants was earliest, and led to the organization of the workers into unions to pit their collective force against the power of their employers.

The favorite device of the unions was collective bargaining enforced by the strike in order to maintain standards of living above the mean competition level. Wherever the unions arose, they were disliked by the employing classes, but as increasing democracy forced the franchise for the workers, they were everywhere able to exert sufficient political pressure to secure complete or partial legalization of union activity.

In England, naturally the first country to see the origin of modern trade unions, they were made illegal by the Combination Acts of 1799 and 1800. Though they received the legal right to exist in 1824 and 1825, all acts which they might perform to give effect to their objects were illegal. After a remarkable outburst of energy between 1830 and 1834, during which the idea of industrial unionism and the general strike were evolved, the first union movement almost disappeared. In the prosperous, expansive years of the middle of the century, English unions revived, but it was soon found, as a result of judicial decisions, that while trade unions were not criminal, they were illegal, their constitutions were nonenforceable contracts, and their officers might embezzle their funds at will.

Since the working classes had just received the right to vote, they used their political power in the next two elections to secure laws which would give their unions the legalization which they desired. Early in the twentieth century the judges again tried to end their existence through a legal decision, when they held in the Taff Vale case that a union was responsible for damages accruing to a company from a strike called against it. But the unions had grown very greatly since 1870, owing to the organization of the unskilled as well as the skilled workers, and the political power of unionism was consequently strong enough to secure the very early rectification of the decision in the Trade Disputes Act of 1906 and the Trade Union Act of 1913.

On the continent the associations of journeymen which reached back to the Middle Ages gradually disappeared before the advance of the factory, and combinations or unions of workingmen were everywhere regarded as illegal. But as industrial conditions altered and circumstances worked together to effect the organization of workers, laws were changed and unions tolerated. In 1884 France gave workers complete freedom of association, and in the midst of the rapid growth of large scale industry after 1890 or 1895 the trade unions or syndicates grew rapidly.

During their early history the French unions had become entangled in the socialist movement and often shared the conflicts and dissensions which tore the French Socialist groups into so many small and hostile fragments. As a result there was no general national association of unions as was represented in England by the Trade Union Congress; rather there was a series of Confédérations, of which the best known outside of France was the Confédération Générale du Travail, the C.G.T., notorious for its revolutionary program and its reliance upon the general strike. But the trade union movement in France numbered only a minority of the workers in 1911, and the C.G.T. only a minority of trade unionists.

In Germany, where industrial development was so slow that craft gilds were not only legal but intact until past the middle of the century, trade unionism did not become a serious question until the burst of progress which coincided with the founding of the empire. By the trade freedom law of 1869, which was extended from the North German Confederation to the empire, unions had the right to exist, but their growth was so slow that in 1895 only 269,000 trade unionists were reported out of a working population of eight million. There was a more rapid growth after 1901; in 1909 there were three million trade unionists organized into three general national alliances, the Free Unions, socialist in tone, the Christian Unions, largely Catholic, and the Hirsch-Dunker Unions with a Liberal outlook.

Remarkable as the development of trade unionism was in all countries, its real advantages and potentialities were discovered by the working classes only in the face of the rising prices of the period 1914–1920; and the modern scope and strength of labor unions to include all workers is really a development of the very recent past.

It should be noted in passing that in addition to trade unionism the working classes of Europe organized other forms of self-help in the face of their growing proletarization. Among the most important of these were cooperative societies of various sorts, particularly societies to save the excessive profits of the ordinary tradesmen in the retail distribution of supplies and food stuffs through the creation of coöperative stores. This sort of coöperation assumed enormous proportions especially in England, where the coöperative retail societies, going back to the Rochdale Pioneers (1844), organized a coöperative wholesale society, which soon owned its own dairies, bakeries, factories, mines, and ships. Cooperative production, on the other hand, was never successful except to a limited extent, under a modified form. In the English cotton spinning factories, for example, groups of workers purchased the stock of the joint stock companies which owned the mills and then continued to operate them through trained technicians like any other corporation.

NOTE: Fuller details of the developments in France and Germany in the nineteenth century may be found in J. H. Clapham, *The Economic Development of France and Germany, 1815–1914,* to which the author desires to express his obligation for certain data used in this chapter.

CHAPTER III

MASS PRODUCTION, IMPERIALISM, AND SOCIAL REFORM, 1875-1927

SINCE the Red Sea is not easily navigable by sailing ships, the opening of the Suez Canal in 1869 led to the scrapping of much of the existing sail tonnage of the world. Shipowners were induced to take advantage of the economies made possible by the compound engine and cheap steel; and, by 1890, Great Britain, for example, had five million tons of steamships in registry. While it was still true that no great nation could import all her food, " a measure of dependence was now possible of which, only a generation earlier, no one had even dreamed."

In the year 1860 the United States had 30,600 miles of railroad; in 1870, 53,300; and in 1880, 84,300. The phenomenal railroad building of these years, particularly in the Mississippi Valley, both resulted from and stimulated the rush to the wheat lands of the northwest. From 1866 to 1871 wheat had stood at top prices, and the export from the United States, hitherto comparatively small, had grown rapidly. Prices of two dollars and more a bushel opened up hundreds of thousands of acres. In 1871 Russian wheat returned to the market, and prices fell to ninety-eight cents a bushel in 1878. With the fall in wheat prices, the only remedy the American farmer could think of was the cultivation of

more wheat; and in the spring of 1878 the valley of the
Red River of the North began to be occupied. Wheat
could be raised on the rich virgin soil and put into
elevators at a cost of $7.50 to $8.50 an acre; a crop of
twenty bushels an acre, sold at seventy-five or eighty-
five cents a bushel, would pay for the land and all expenses the first year.

With adequate railroad facilities and cheap ocean
freights, made possible by the enormous recent steamship construction, the American farmer began to dump
his wheat into Europe at prices lower than the production costs of crops raised on the comparatively poor
soil of England and the continent.

In 1873 a cargo of frozen meat was shipped from
Australia to London. It was spoiled when it arrived.
European agriculture, already threatened by the American wheat farmer, was still protected from the menace
of the Australasian grazier. In 1880 the steamer *Strath-
leven*, fitted with a Bell-Coleman refrigerating machine,
brought a second cargo of frozen meat from Australia
to London. It arrived in prime condition. Although
it was still possible to assert that the flavor of English
meat was better, it was not long before Canterbury
(New Zealand, not England) mutton graced the dinner
tables of even respectable English families.

The net result of these developments was a stupendous increase in the amount of food available for European consumption and the creation of a series of reactions upon population and industry similar in their
ultimate effects to those brought about by earlier increases in the available supplies of food and other basic

materials. Yet under the existing social structure of European life, all was not clear gain, since the flooding of Europe with cheap grain and cheap meat was accompanied by complicated reactions upon the European agricultural populations, and sharp readjustments in national policy, which make it possible to date the last phase of the Industrial Revolution from this time.

In consequence of the new food supplies several effects were possible. The agricultural interests might be able to secure tariff protection and thus save themselves. During the course of the age of coal and iron the older mercantilistic protective regulations which hedged in European commerce, industry, and agriculture had been rather generally abandoned. Great Britain took the lead by repealing the Corn Laws in 1846, the Navigation Acts in 1849, and the remaining protective tariff schedules by 1860. Prussia had begun the work for Germany by the formation of the Zollverein in 1828, by which internal free trade within the Zollverein territory was assured and only very moderate duties levied on imports. France had revised her tariff sharply downward in 1860, in consequence of the Cobden Treaty between France and England, and, in a general way, most nations of Europe adopted free trade or very low tariffs at about this time. But with the agricultural crisis of the later 1870's, European statesmen began to wonder whether they had not been the " dupes of an amiable error "; and, under the pressure of the powerful aristocracy, especially if the manufacturing interests also felt the lure of higher prices, they were in some cases induced to begin upward revisions of their tariffs. This was preëminently the situation in France and in Germany, where tariff barriers were set up so high in the 'eighties and 'nineties, that agriculture held its own both in grain farming and meat production, and still does so.

Such countries as Denmark and Holland saved themselves by practically abandoning wheat farming, and turning to dairying and other highly specialized forms of agriculture. The high degree of popular education in these lands, where nearly everyone is coming to have a high school training, may account for the alertness, initiative, and enterprise of the people, which have made possible not only a fundamental revision of methods, but the creation of coöperative agricultural societies and agencies on a more complete scale than anywhere else in the world.

The English agriculturalists would have liked to adopt measures similar to those of France and Germany, and they have not yet abandoned hope of eventual success. In the 'eighties, however, they feared to suggest the subject seriously as a matter of practical politics, (although many books were written upon the question), because of the faith of the manufacturers in free trade and the eagerness of the masses for cheap food. When the Conservatives tried to make the idea more palatable in 1906 and 1910 by linking it with the question of closer imperial unity, they were defeated in the general elections; and they had no better success when they tried to arouse subsidiary enthusiasm over the necessity of protecting "key industries" in 1921 and 1923.

In view of the failure of the movement for agricultural protection in England, two other courses were open. Certain soils were preëminently suited for dairy farming, and for small fruits and truck; and where the squire could stand the wrench of seeing his land grow strawberries instead of wheat, profits might still be made. But if wheat was the only possible crop for reasons of sentiment, soil, or geography, the poorer lands might be allowed to go out of cultivation, the rents of others would be reduced, and the landowner, the farmer, and the agricultural laborer would find themselves with reduced incomes and lowered living standards. This course was actually followed in many places in England, and the consequent loss of capital and profits in English agriculture between 1875 and 1905 was estimated at £1600 millions. There was a general destruction of enterprise, the wheat area began to contract, land was allowed to revert to rough pasture, and improvements, such as drainage, were arrested.

The immediate situation in the late 'seventies and early 'eighties was made worse by the reaction of a series of European and American wars, the payment of the indemnity by France to Germany, overdevelopment in American railroads, speculation in securities, and financial crises.

THE REVIVAL OF IMPERIALISM

To make good the losses in purchasing power of the agricultural elements, until then the largest single consuming group in British life, it was necessary to cultivate overseas markets more extensively than ever before. Moreover, since these proved unable to absorb by direct purchase all the excess British output of manufactured goods, it was essential, in order to maintain profits, returns on capital, wages, and prices at home, by keeping the British factories running to capacity, to lay down vast quantities of goods as investments. This process had already been going on since the early part of the nineteenth century, and English manufacturers had already learned the value of such colonial markets as India, which absorbed nearly half the annual output of British cotton goods, and had provided a field for the building of over five thousand miles of railroad from British materials before 1875. Colonial development was pushed with extraordinary vigor after 1875 or 1880, to effect a revival of business from the slump created by the decline in the purchasing power of agriculture, and the period of the modern economic imperialism was begun. While Great Britain inevitably played the greatest rôle in the export of capital, other countries also embarked upon imperialistic ventures. The subsequent rivalry for "colonies" is one of the most significant developments of the new period.

Through the explorations of Caille, Ruppel and Burckhardt, and Speke, Baker, and Livingstone, through the showy extravagance of Ismail, Khedive of Egypt, and through the extraordinary journey of Henry M. Stanley to find Livingstone, Africa had got upon the front page during the third quarter of the nineteenth century. The dark continent now seized upon the imaginations of British and European commercial and industrial leaders as possessing infinite possibilities of exploitation of the sort now necessary to provide markets to keep their factories running full time.

The first man really to sense the situation was Leopold II of Belgium, who, in addition to being a king in his public capacity, was in private life a very shrewd business man. After taking Stanley into his employ to continue the exploration of the Congo basin, Leopold called a congress of the powers in 1876 to discuss the civilization of Africa, the "means of opening up the interior of the continent to the commerce, industry, and scientific enterprise of the civilized world," and the extirpation of "the terrible scourge of slavery." As a result of the deliberations of this assembly, the International African Association was formed. This presently became the International Association of the Congo, under the cover of which Leopold employed Stanley to stake out, by means of treaties with the natives and by founding stations, a vast colony in the Congo region. When the Portuguese, who had ancient claims in Africa, began to resent the encroachments which were being made upon their own territory, Leopold subtly confused his public and private capacities, and induced the powers of Europe, in the Berlin Congress of 1884–5, to sanction his enterprise under the name of the Congo Free State. Of this Leopold was not only sovereign but owner and entrepreneur.

Other business men, not themselves sovereigns, had to adopt other methods to secure the same opportunities for African enterprise and activity. Their agents, like

Stanley, staked out the limits of their fields of operation by treaties with the native chiefs, and in these areas they at once began to make investments. As soon as they had established themselves, they approached their governments to give them support, especially against the capitalists of other countries who might also be interested in the same districts. If the pressure which the various business interests could bring to bear was great enough, their governments might be induced to give them charters authorizing their activity, and, at the same time, to approach the other governments of Europe through diplomatic channels and arrange for the allotment of areas between their nationals. In this way Sir George Goldie, Sir William Mackinnon, Adolf Luderitz, and Cecil Rhodes, and their associates formed the Royal Niger Company, and the other chartered companies which divided central Africa among themselves in the decade of the 1880's.

While imperialism was the direct consequence of the necessity for immediate readjustments created by the agricultural crisis and attendant business depression of the later 'seventies and early 'eighties, the continuance of imperialistic expansion all through the period and the participation of even those countries where agriculture was restored to its former standing indicate that the agricultural depression was not the only factor, and that industrial developments must also be considered as fundamental. As time went on, the high pressure drive for new markets to absorb the rapidly increasing industrial output became the really significant factor in the situation.

In this connection a few apparently isolated facts may be used to provide illustrations of really significant progress.

Typical Advances in Medicine

In the decade between 1890 and 1900 bacteriologists discovered the antitoxins of tetanus and cholera, and in 1901 Dr. Emil A. von Behring, director of the Hygienic Institute at Marburg, received the Nobel prize for an antitoxin of diphtheria, which he improved in 1913. In 1900 Dr. Walter Reed of the United States Army demonstrated that yellow fever was carried only by the *Stegomyia fasciata* mosquito, and within a few years yellow fever was almost extinct. At the same time Dr. Almroth Wright of London worked out a vaccine for typhoid. Early in 1911 Dr. Paul Ehrlich and his associate, Dr. Hata, announced the discovery of salvarsan, an organic arsenic compound, which when injected into the body destroyed syphilis germs, without deleterious effect on other organisms or bodily functions.

Characteristic New Basic Materials

On the 28th of August, 1859, the tools with which E. L. Drake was drilling for oil in western Pennsylvania suddenly dropped into a crevice, and the next day the well was found to have struck petroleum. Twelve years later drilling began all over the world. The Galician and Roumanian fields were first tapped in 1878 and 1880; those of Sumatra, Java, and Borneo between

1883 and 1896, and those of Burma in 1890. In 1914 arrangements were made to apportion the most recently discovered, still unexploited fields in the Tigro-Euphrates valley.

Near the close of the Second Empire, Napoleon III offered a prize for the best substitute for butter. It was won in 1869 by Hippolyte Mége-Mouries, who made oleomargerine by churning oleo oil and other fatty substances together with milk. His process made available for human food not only beef suet, from which oleo oil was extracted, but, still more important, the cocoanut oil which the South Sea Islands were capable of producing in large quantities. The subsequent study of the chemistry of vegetable oils gave to the various palm and nut oils of Africa a significant place as industrial materials.

In 1824 Joseph Aspdin, a bricklayer of Leeds, took out a patent for a cement which he called Portland cement, because, when hard, its texture resembled that of Portland stone. In 1867 J. F. Monier, a French gardener, used iron bars to strengthen the cement in making basins for fountains. In 1884, through the publication of *Das System Monier*, the owners of the German rights of Monier's patent spread the rapid use of ferroconcrete or reinforced concrete for structural purposes.

Rubber had been known in Europe since the later eighteenth century, and considerable quantities were used in Europe and the United States after 1844 when Charles Goodyear patented his process of vulcanization with sulphur, which made rubber practicable for rubber overshoes. Yet it did not become a really important commodity of world trade until Charles Dunlop used it in 1883 for the construction of a pneumatic tire for bicycles. Twelve years later it was used to make automobile tires.

Coal tar, the black, evil smelling, sticky residue which remained in retorts after coal had been distilled for illuminating gas had occupied the attention of chemists long before 1850, and in 1846 and 1847 English and German investigators worked out methods for its distillation. In 1856 W. H. Perkins produced a purple dye from coal tar and discovered the first aniline color. In 1868 Graebe and Liebermann astounded the chemical world by preparing alizarine, the coloring principle of madder root, from the anthracene of coal tar. In 1880 Baeyer produced indigo synthetically from coal tar products.

Among the most essential of chemicals in fertilizers are the nitrates, such as ammonia and its salts. In the later nineteenth century, Europe and America imported nitrates in extraordinary quantities from Chile, where natural deposits of hundreds of square miles in area are found. But the early twentieth century was already beginning to fear the exhaustion of the Chilean supply. There would, of course, be no question of shortage of nitrates if the nitrogen of the air could be " fixed," that is, caught and combined with hydrogen or some base so that it might be made available in agriculture and industry also. Just before 1914 Haber succeeded in making synthetic ammonia by passing highly compressed hydrogen and nitrogen through heated chambers in the presence of a catalyst, and nitric acid was formed directly from the air by the action of high tension arcs on air passing through them. Immense factories were erected in 1913 at Oppau and Merse-burg in Germany where 100,000 tons of ammonia were made in 1917; and after the war the new process was introduced into the allied countries.

Finally among the new essential materials must be mentioned the rare earths and metals, such as osmium, thorium, tantalum, chromium, tungsten, and others, which are of the greatest consequence in the electrical and steel industries.

Improvements in Prime Motors (Engines)

In the 1850's the single expansion steam engine was provided with a second, larger cylinder in which the steam was expanded a second time. In this way more of the energy of the steam was used, and the efficiency of the engine almost doubled. Working at 60 pounds pressure the compound engine consumed three and one-half pounds of coal per horse power per hour. In 1874 A. C. Kirk invented the triple expansion engine, which came into general use about 1881. At 150 to 200 pounds steam pressure this engine used only one and one-half pounds of coal per horse power per hour. In 1894 came the quadruple expansion engine, working at 225 pounds steam pressure with a coal consumption of one and one-quarter pounds per horse power per hour.

The comparatively slight reduction effected by the addition of the fourth cylinder indicated that the expansion steam engine had reached the limit of perfectibility. Other possible types of engine were, therefore, investigated, in which the kinetic, as well as the expansive, force of steam might be employed by utilizing something like the principle of the water wheel. Between 1884 and 1897 Mr. C. A. Parsons invented and developed the steam turbine, the limits of the size and efficiency of which have not been reached even yet. The turbine installations in the *Mauretania* and *Lusitania* were 70,000 horse power; those in recently constructed generating stations approach 200,000 horse power.

In 1876 Dr. N. A. Otto invented the first successful internal combustion engine. It worked at a speed of 150 to 200 revolutions per minute. In 1883 Gottlieb Daimler hit upon the idea of a very small engine with light parts, which should attain the same horse power as the heavy Otto engine by lessening the impulses but increasing the speed to 800 to 1000 revolutions per minute. When George Benz of Mannheim replaced the hot tube, by means of which the gas had been ignited, with an electric spark, the modern racing engine was, in its essentials, complete.

In 1897 Rudolf Diesel perfected an internal combustion engine using crude oil as a fuel in which the ignition of the gases was brought about by very high compression, of from four or five hundred pounds to the square inch in the cylinders. The efficiency of this engine excited the greatest interest. Three tons thirteen hundred weight of oil costing twelve dollars delivered more power through a Diesel engine than twelve tons fifteen hundred weight of coal costing fifty dollars burned under a steam boiler. In consequence Diesel engine installation grew rapidly in those countries where there was the requisite mechanical skill and patience to build the rather intricate mechanism; and in 1922 the the use of the Diesel engine at sea had progressed so far that a 20,000 ton Diesel engine steamer was ordered by the Union Steamship Company of New Zealand.

Equally significant as the development of internal combustion engines in the latest age of the Industrial Revolution was the perfection of the electric dynamo and the electric motor, which is simply a dynamo reversed. While the principle of the dynamo was discovered in 1831 by Michael Faraday, it was not until 1867 that Werner von Siemens built a working dynamo which made it possible to produce electricity in any desired quantity. The first generating stations were built for light, but after the demonstration at the Frankfurt Exposition in 1891 of the possibilities of the transmission of power over long distances, electric tramway or trolley line construction went forward very rapidly in all countries. At about the same time the electric motor began to be used for driving machinery; and its introduction made it possible for many small workshops which still remained in such trades as cutlery-making to hold their own in competition with the larger factories.

In conjunction with the water turbine and high tension transmission systems, the dynamo has made possible in the twentieth century the utilization of water power in ever greater measure. At present one of the largest installations sends 150,000 kilowatts 240 miles from the Sierras to Los Angeles; power will soon be transmitted from Norway to Copenhagen; and a project is in hand for the transmission of 200,000 kilowatts 700 miles from the Victoria Falls on the Zambesi to points in the Union of South Africa.

Progress in Transportation

In 1875 India had something over five thousand miles of railway line; Egypt, seven hundred odd miles; Australasia, thirteen hundred miles; and Cape Colony, one hundred and thirty-four miles. The bulk of the remainder of the mileage of the world, which came to a total of 165,000 miles of line, was in western Europe and the United States. In 1925 every continent had its complement of railroads. The total world mileage was over 700,000 miles of line and of this a large part of the new construction had been in Asia, Africa, and Australia.

In 1875 the ship tonnage of the world was approximately 15,000,000 tons; in 1925, 64,000,000. The first ship to exceed 10,000 tons, apart from the abortive *Great Eastern* of the later 'fifties, was the *City of Paris*, built in 1888; in 1899 the *Oceanic* first exceeded 15,000 tons; in 1901 the *Celtic* passed the 20,000 ton mark; and in 1907 the *Mauretania* and *Lusitania* went above 30,000 tons for the first time. The *Majestic*, built between 1914 and 1921, at present the world's largest ship, has a registered tonnage of 56,551 tons. Just as the crack liners have tended to become larger and, incidentally, faster, the cargo ships have also tended to increase in size and speed, from an average of

2,000 tons in 1890 to 8,000 or 10,000 tons in the most recent period, and from seven to ten knots an hour.

In 1886 Daimler attached his light racing engine already described to a bicycle, and on March 4, 1887 he drove his first motor car through the streets of Hanover. In the same year Messrs. Panhard and Levassor, then engaged in making wood-working machinery in Paris, were attracted by an exhibit of Daimler's racing motor at the Paris Exhibition and purchased the French rights for its use. Their great contribution was the development of a transmission system for use in the new horseless carriage for which they foresaw a brilliant future.

In 1895 an automobile race was run from Paris to Bordeaux and return, 744 miles. The winner averaged 15 miles per hour.

In 1896 the English locomotive law, which prohibited the passage of self-propelled vehicles on highways at more than four miles an hour and required that a man carrying a red flag should precede every such vehicle, was repealed.

The light motor made possible not only the automobile but the airplane. In 1903 Wilbur and Orville Wright added a small light motor to the glider with which they were experimenting and they remained in the air fifty-nine seconds. Two years later they flew twenty-four and one-half miles in half an hour. On September 9, 1908 Orville Wright made three public flights at Fort Myer, Virginia; four days later Wilbur Wright, in France, flew fifty-six miles in one hour, thirty-one minutes, twenty-five and four-fifths seconds.

On July 25, 1909 L. Bleriot flew from Calais to Dover in thirty-one minutes. Early in 1918 regular airplane passenger service was opened between Berlin and Cologne.

Developments in Communication

On June 25, 1875, while experimenting with his " harmonic telegraph," Alexander Graham Bell distinctly heard the twang of a spring, which on inquiry he found that his assistant in the next room had snapped. He recognized instantly that he had discovered a device for the transmission of sounds, not mere signals. On March 10, 1876 the first articulate sentence was heard over the new telephone, and at the Centennial Exposition of 1876 in Philadelphia thousands marveled at the new magic.

In 1896 Signor G. Marconi gave practical form to certain theoretical knowledge and succeeded in sending an electric signal without wires. Later experiments were carried on in England, the distances were gradually increased, and in 1901 it was decided to make the attempt to cross the Atlantic. On December 12, 1901 Marconi, at his receiving station at St. John's, Newfoundland, repeatedly heard the letter " S " at the times he had prearranged for its sending from his transmission station at Poldhu in Cornwall. Transatlantic wireless was a fact.

The wireless telephone was but a development of the wireless telegraph. In 1927 wireless telephone service between London and New York and other American cities was opened to the public.

New Speed Records

In 1890 the fastest scheduled time of the fastest British trains was 54.12 miles an hour; in 1900 it was 59.09 miles an hour; and in 1910, 61.7 miles an hour.

In 1873 the *Baltic* held the record for the North Atlantic passage by a crossing in seven days, twenty hours, and nine minutes. In 1888 the *City of Paris* cut the time to under six days. In 1903 the *Deutschland* made a record of under five and one-half days, and in 1910 the *Mauretania* won the blue ribbon of the Atlantic, which she still holds, by a crossing in four days, ten hours, and forty-one minutes.

In October, 1924, the Zeppelin ZR–3, now the *Los Angeles,* flew from Friedrichshafen to Lakehurst, 5066 miles, in eighty-one hours, seventeen minutes.

On June 14–15, 1919, Captain Alcock and Lieutenant Brown flew in a biplane from St. John's, Newfoundland, to Clifden, Ireland, 1960 miles, in sixteen hours and twelve minutes.

On May 2–3, 1923, Lieutenants John Macready and Oakley J. Kelly, in the United States Army monoplane T2, flew from Mineola, New York, to San Diego, California, 2520 miles, in twenty-six hours, fifty minutes, thirty-eight and two-fifths seconds.

On October 12, 1925, Cyrus Bettis flew 200 kilometres for the Pulitzer trophy at the rate of 248 miles per hour.

In general outlines the progress in industry of the period after 1875 or 1880 was in the same general direction as that of the age of coal and iron, but everything was on a strikingly larger scale. The Industrial Revolution itself spread far beyond western Europe and industrialized not only the United States but Japan, besides the smaller states of Europe, such as Italy, the Scandinavian countries, and parts of eastern Europe. Populations were larger than ever; and, though the birth-rate fell sharply in some countries, the death-rate was also lowered through the marvellous achievements of medical science. Many new materials were added to the essential supplies upon which civilized life was based, and their production was in certain cases made independent of natural stores by synthetic chemical and physical processes. Improvements in design and the adoption of new principles revolutionized the efficiency of the steam engine, and the electric dynamo and motor and the internal combustion engine turned the energy of water power and oil to the service of man.

The tendency toward increasing speed in living, which has already been noticed in the earlier periods, was stimulated tremendously by the improvements in transportation and communication. The development had its psychological aspects in the substitution of the short story for the novel, of the movie for the play; its emotional reactions were revealed in the restless temper of modern society which would make a lifetime altogether too long for many people for a single romance and love experience; artistically, the pursuit of speed culminated in the ever more rapid movement of music and the dance from syncopation and the two step through rag time and jazz, the fox trot and the Charleston, reaching its apotheosis in the blues and the blackbottom.

KARTELLS AND TRUSTS

Economically, the higher speed of life together with the lessening of the time and cost factor in distance resulted in greater and more rapid turnover and exchange, and business men were enabled to spread their markets over wider areas. As a consequence industrial enterprises developed larger producing units; and more extensive factories with better equipment were built. Firms which had hitherto manufactured for a single locality enlarged to supply a nation; companies which already had national markets entered international trade. After a brief period of intense and bitter rivalry which resulted when the expanding companies came into competition with each other in the larger areas, the advantages of agreements, apportionments of output and markets, and amalgamation came to be recognized. This was especially the case as the weaker companies were eliminated.

In Germany the movement took the form of the organization of Kartells or associations of companies engaged in the same lines of business, with a view to maintaining prices, fixing output, and apportioning markets. In England and the United States the trust movement was the more common result. Plants engaged in particular lines of production all over the country were brought together under common control; and to the economies effected in production in the larger individual units which this process made possible were added those accruing from the reduction of overhead through the elimination of numerous managements.

Through this development such vast industrial aggregates as the Imperial Tobacco Company, J. and P. Coats (the Cotton Thread Trust), and Bryant and May (the Match Trust) came into existence in England at just about the beginning of the twentieth century, and in the financial world the process was duplicated in the amalgamation of hundreds of smaller banks into the great joint stock banks, such as Lloyds Bank, the London Joint City and Midland Bank, the National Provincial and Union Bank, Barclay's Bank, and the London County Westminster and Parr's Bank. The increased output of industry as a result of these developments is shown in the figures for the British national income. In 1883 the total national income was estimated at £1200 million; in 1910 it was about £2000 million, in spite of the losses in agriculture which resulted from the period of agricultural depression.

THE TENDENCY TOWARD INTERNATIONAL INDUSTRIAL ORGANIZATIONS

The tendency toward industrial expansion and amalgamation did not stop at national frontiers, but manifested itself in international and worldwide forms. Companies might so enlarge their business as to have branches in many parts of the world, or agreements, pools, and even outright amalgamations might be effected between important groups of different countries. Thus the Nobel Trust, a Norwegian concern, made the world's dynamite; the Solvay syndicate, a Belgian corporation, dominated the production of soda. The General Electric Company of the United States and the

Allgemeine Elektrizitäts Gesellschaft, the A.E.G., of Germany had working agreements with each other, and the A.E.G. had a subsidiary in South America which controlled the electrical appliances market in that continent. The American Tobacco Company secured a large interest in the Imperial Tobacco Company of Great Britain, it worked in Germany, and in association with the Imperial Tobacco Company, under the form of the British-American Tobacco Company, it competed for the trade of the rest of the world. In every important trade area, excepting in the freight traffic of the North Atlantic, the various shipping companies in each area arranged " conferences," which fixed rates and apportioned and even pooled business. The International Steel Rail Syndicate included the steel rail manufacturers of Great Britain, Germany, France, Belgium, and the United States, and divided the export trade of the world among the manufacturers of the various nations.

These are but examples of the several hundred international associations and companies of various kinds in world industry which came into existence in the period before 1914. While the war brought many of these to an end, the process of their formation was resumed after the war, and is represented in the more recent past by the agreements of the French and German potash producers, who scarcely waited for the Treaty of Versailles, and those of the German and French steel manufacturers. Industrial capital truly ceased to have a country where questions of greater efficiency or greater profits were at stake.

RECENT IMPERIALISM

The progress of production here sketched not only made industry responsible for some of the economic imperialism of the period after 1875 or 1880, but led to renewed activity in imperialistic ventures after 1900. Each year, owing to the growing perfection of industrial processes, there was a larger surplus of production which could not be used at home. If industry was to be kept running at full time, it was more than ever requisite that effective demand for the surplus goods should be created; and as society was organized the effective demand most capable of being cultivated was in the so-called more backward nations, where extensive opportunities for the disposal of European goods existed if the peoples could be induced to accept the mechanical civilization of Europe.

Lacking railroads, bridges, telephones, telegraphs, electric lights, water supply systems, and other similar devices, Morocco, Egypt, Asiatic Turkey, Persia, Siam, China, and Korea could absorb the European surplus and even stimulate further production. Since these countries were in no position to make cash payment for the material goods which formed the apparatus of western civilization which was now being extended to them, the bankers, who handled the financial end of the export of capital, demanded guarantees and concessions which in effect reduced one after another of these lands to colonies of the various European powers.

An important but subsidiary impulse in the imperialistic spirit of the twentieth century was the growing fear of the shortage of raw materials, coupled with the realization that, in so far as the areas of production were in the hands of the less mechanically advanced peoples, the most efficient methods were not being followed. To achieve the greatest possible yield it was held justifiable to occupy the less efficiently exploited districts and enforce better methods. Ideas of this sort gained particular currency in countries in which the demand for certain products was especially active, as, for instance, oil in Great Britain during the war, or rubber in the United States after the war. If the desire to augment the supplies of raw materials involved capital investments of large amounts, the most important developments might follow.

It must be kept in mind, of course, that this whole development represents merely the economic basis of imperialism, and that its political expression, the annexation of colonies and the proclamation of spheres of influence, was dependent upon a number of other factors, such as the general foreign policy of the European governments, the domestic political situation, strategic considerations, and the personalities of the officials who controlled the European foreign offices. In a general way, however, in the last analysis, the meat and matter of nearly all foreign policy in the early twentieth century was the privileges and rights of the various nationals of Europe in the colonial areas of the world.

As a result of the whole complex of forces thus engaged Morocco became a French colony, except for the northern Mediterranean coast, which for certain strategic considerations was assigned to Spain; Tunis went to France; Tripoli was seized by Italy. Great Britain's exclusive rights in Egypt were acknowledged; and Germany had practically succeeded in annexing Turkey as a result of an agreement with Great Britain which provided for the construction of the Bagdad railway by the Germans and the allotment of three-fourths of the oil of the Tigro-Euphrates valley to the British. Persia was divided between Russia and Great Britain; Siam, between France and Great Britain; Korea went to Japan; and China only escaped public division because the United States, not included in any arrangements which might have been made already, insisted upon the open door.

THE MOVEMENT FOR SOCIAL REFORM

The mechanization of the world and the spread of European appliances of transportation, communication, and production to the most remote and backward regions may ultimately result in the universal quickening of life to something like European levels, and the consequent increase in production and consumption among all peoples to something like the intensity of Europe. If European control over the heavy exports of capital which are making this consummation possible remains intact, the world will pay a handsome annual tribute to Europe for her earlier activity, which may possibly accrue to the advantage of all classes in European society.

Until the process comes into full bearing, however, the vast investments of European capital in the less advanced regions of Africa and Asia unquestionably have subtracted from the amount of goods potentially available for consumption at home. This was early recognized in many quarters in the various western European countries, where it was held that the immediate ends achieved by imperialism could better be attained by more careful cultivation of the graces of life at home. The same effective demand which Morocco, under proper stimulus, exercised for harbor works and railroads could be created at home by increasing the consuming power of the great masses of the population. Morocco might have to remain untouched by the blessings of western civilization, but the East End of London could be made a better and happier place to live in.

The most direct way of increasing domestic consuming power lay in raising wages, but wage levels were considered so complicated a problem as to be altogether outside the scope of social control, except in certain very special cases. Those who urged concentration on the development of each country's own inner possibilities as the more desirable social policy were led, therefore, to insist upon programs of social reform, under which the state seized the social surplus in the form of taxes and distributed it to the masses in such direct benefits as better education, better houses, more recreational facilities, insurance against sickness and unemployment, and old age pensions.

While such ideas were quite foreign to the philosophy of the *laissez faire* politicians who carried over into the twentieth the notions of the early nineteenth century, they had already laid the groundwork for such a policy in their various labor and factory laws. These the workers in England first succeeded in winning partly by their own appeals to popular emotion and their tales of the horrors of child labor, and partly in consequence of the Conservative desire for vengeance upon the factory owners for the repeal of the Corn Laws in 1846. As the result of the legislation of the nineteenth century child labor in England was prohibited, the hours of young persons and women legally limited to ten a day, and those of men practically fixed by this limitation. It was made possible to bring any industry under the scope of regulatory legislation by listing it as a dangerous trade, and, early in the twentieth century, the sweated worker, economically the most helpless member of the industrial hierarchy, was actually assured the payment of a minimum wage. In 1870 Gladstone, the most uncompromising adherent of the *laissez faire* creed, assented to the provision of a state system of education; and, as was pointed out almost immediately, if the state could provide education, there was now no logical reason why the state should not provide its people with anything and everything.

The next step in the direction of the socialistic projects advanced in the twentieth century was taken by Bismarck in Germany. Finding that his repressive measures for the destruction of socialism exercised under the Exceptional Law of 1878 only added to the numbers of those who accepted the gospel of socialism which Karl Marx enunciated from his seat in the reading room of the British Museum, Bismarck determined to disarm the socialist movement by adopting its own measures. He was never much concerned with factory laws, since the conditions of excessive competition between workers for jobs, which resulted in the long hours and low wages of the English factories and were at the basis of English legislation, did not prevail in Prussia. He was more concerned with protecting the workingman from sickness, accident, unemployment, old age, and other vicissitudes of life under modern industrial conditions, which seemed to him responsible for the misfortune and therefore the discontent of his people. He would have liked to develop a most comprehensive insurance scheme for this purpose, and while he never tackled unemployment insurance, he did much with other varieties. In 1883, sickness insurance was instituted; in 1884, accident insurance; and in 1885, old age and invalidity insurance. By 1911, 13,600,000 people in Germany were insured against sickness and invalidity, and in that year extensions of the protected classes were made to include domestic servants, agricultural workers, casual laborers, and salaried persons as well as workers in industry.

Under all these schemes contributions were made by the individual, his employer, and the state; and the popularity of the protection thus made available was so great that even the socialists, who had denounced the code as an attempt to reconcile workingmen with the existing state of society and the empire, came to look upon them as " foundation walls " upon which even socialists might build.

With the growing political power of the proletarian masses in the early twentieth century, achieved through their organization in political parties, it became req-

uisite for governments to consider seriously the demands for social reform if only to prevent more radical
proposals. The most far-reaching concessions were
those made in England, where both the Conservatives
and the Liberals were genuinely concerned with the alle-
viation of the problem of poverty, which had been
revealed by the unemployment situation of the late
'eighties, and placed in the clearest light by the researches of Charles Booth, William Booth, Seebohm
Rowntree, and other sociological investigators. The
Conservatives believed that the remedy lay in a high
protective tariff, which would shut out the manufactures
of other countries, and so stimulate demand for British
goods, as well as in the imperialistic program of cultivating markets in colonial areas which was already being followed.

The Liberals, and particularly that wing of the party
known as Little Englanders, led by David Lloyd George
and John Morley, men inspired by genuine humani-
tarian feelings, presented a program of far-reaching
significance. It provided for an elaborate scheme of
social insurance, including benefits in sickness, unemployment, and old age; it sought to compel landowners
to break up their estates to provide small holdings for
the agricultural laborers and cheap building lots for the
urban workers; and it envisaged the destruction of the
slums and the creation of garden cities. In the schools
and even kindergartens of the state healthy children,
regularly inspected by a state physician, and provided,
if necessary, with lunches by the state if they showed
evidences of lack of proper food at home, should learn

the art of living until they reached at least their four-
teenth or sixteenth years.

To ease the problem of underemployment and casual
work, an elaborate system of labor exchanges, or state
employment agencies, was established, to furnish information to workers needing employment and to masters
requiring help, so that workers in seasonal trades might
know where their services were most in demand when
they were laid off in slack times.   To deal with great
unemployment crises it was even suggested that a ten
year program of public works, such as land reclamation
and harbor improvements, be adopted and planned, to
be set in operation as soon as trade depression began, to
absorb those laid off in industry and to revive business
activity by the demands thus created.

The cost of all these projects was wholly or partly
borne by the state.   Since the most dreaded prospect of
the proletarian population was penniless old age, and
since, moreover, it was estimated that 30 per cent of all
pauperism was due to sickness, it is probably true that
the most direct benefits of the Liberal program were the
old age pensions, which the state paid in their entirety,
and the protection of sickness and unemployment insurance, to which the state made large contributions.

While the total costs of the various German and
English social reform measures were very large in the
twentieth century, those who felt that the social surplus
could be diverted from imperialistic projects and de-
voted to the advantage of the working classes through
various state benefits must have been bitterly disillu-
sioned when they found that the surplus exported in

England, for example, was much greater in 1912 than it had been in 1906 when the Liberal party had come into office. British investments abroad increased from £104.4 millions a year in 1906 to £226 millions a year in 1912, and the same sort of rapid rise was found in the foreign investments of France, Germany, Austria, and other nations.

More than that, by 1911 or 1912 the peoples of Europe ceased to be satisfied with what had been done for them, as they began to discover that in spite of all beneficial legislation, their wages were buying less than they had purchased ten years earlier. Europe was in the midst of a price revolution, partly the result of excessive investments abroad which were not yet yielding their full return, and partly the result of the gradual slowing down of the rate of acceleration of production and the beginning of a period of stabilization in European industry. Prices had begun to rise just before the new century began, and by the end of the first decade the effects were being felt. Everywhere in Europe there was discontent, which expressed itself in various ways. Sometimes details of government social policy were sharply criticized, as, for example, certain provisions of the National Insurance Act in England in 1911; more generally very severe strikes on a larger scale than was previously known broke out.

Before the movement could really orient itself and develop a program, the World War swept over Europe, bringing with it not only the introduction of the automatic machine which deprived the skilled laborer of his preferential position in industry, but also the high war time prices which threatened existing living standards. The result was the universal strengthening of labor organizations (although some of the older types of organization lost their hold for the moment) and the attainment by the working classes of wages, conditions of labor, hours, and standards of living better than those which prevailed in 1914. Labor even won what had never been seriously considered as a possibility in 1914, the right to share in industrial management and control. Since the old governing classes lost their grip everywhere in the height of the war, they were unable with the coming of peace to restore the situation as it had been when the war started. While they were generally successful in reasserting the control of industry by the employer or the technician, they could not restore hours, wages, or living standards of the prewar period.

THE EFFECTS OF THE INDUSTRIAL REVOLUTION

Writing in 1847, when the Industrial Revolution had only started, John Stuart Mill pessimistically remarked: " Hitherto it is questionable if all the mechanical inventions yet made have lightened the day's toil of any human being. They have enabled a greater population to live the same life of drudgery and imprisonment." In one of his more bitter moments a philosopher of to-day might repeat Mill's observation. He would be compelled to add, however, that not only was there a greater population, but that each individual had a larger share of material goods than was possible in early days when the numbers of people were much smaller.

Statistical evidence indicates that the totals of wealth of the present time are without comparison greater than they were in the past, and that men are in the aggregate better housed, better clothed and fed, provided with better care and attention in sickness, and better educated, no matter how that term may be defined, than in the past. They have more leisure also, and the eight hour day is so nearly attained in western Europe and America that enthusiasts, such as Lord Leverhulme and Henry Ford, are already talking about a four hour day or a five day week. While it is undeniably true that the great masses are still not adepts in the noble uses of that leisure which they have, even here advances have been made, and there is surely no comparison between the sadistic " fighting up and down " of early nineteenth century Lancashire and the enthusiastically welcomed program of a Welsh choir in the present, to take extreme cases.

Happiness does not consist in the abundance of material possessions, yet it is also true that in this life, at least, free spiritual activity is conditioned by the enjoyment of a certain minimum of material wealth. As a result of the Industrial Revolution the masses of western European peoples are more favorably situated in the matter of the enjoyment of the essential minimum than ever in history: it is not yet sure that their prosperity will lead to happiness. Only this much is certain. It is no longer possible to see a woman working in the fields of western Europe in October clad only in an old open coat, a skirt, and nothing else.

How far the social processes set in motion by the

Industrial Revolution will continue their development is not a question for the historian. There are, however, certain indications that as far as western Europe is concerned, the most rapid changes in industry are a thing of the past. The birth-rate of all European peoples has fallen greatly in recent decades. While this is in part to be attributed to the spread of the knowledge of birth control, and the determination of the masses to use that knowledge to safeguard their recently won standards of living, it would not be necessary for them to follow this course if the acceleration in production were as rapid as it was in the period ending approximately in the 1890's or early 1900's. While output is still increasing all along the line, the law of diminishing returns seems to be at work in such basic essential supplies as British coal, American wheat, and other materials upon the more rapid exploitation of which the upward tendency in population depended. Already the Victorian dream of human perfectibility based upon a more complete and absolute control by man over the forces of nature is dissipated.

Another factor, which may prove significant for the future, is the tendency of the Industrial Revolution to spread beyond western Europe and the United States to the white colonies of the world, such as the dominions of the British Empire, and even to the populous nations of dark-skinned races. If the development of industrialism among such people as the Chinese, for example, should be accompanied by anything like the rise in standards of living which attended the Industrial Revolution in Europe, there might be a sharp curtailment of

essential supplies available for Europe, or a long drawn-
out warfare to control such supplies. Yet the future
which holds such problems in store may also unlock the
secret of synthetic foods to solve them.

Whatever may be true of the more remote future, at
the moment the limits of the reduction of the time and
cost factors in distance do not seem to have been
reached. Still higher speed in living is indicated by
such exploits as the flight of Captain Charles Lindbergh
from New York to Paris on May 20-21, 1927, in thirty-
three hours and thirty-two minutes. The serenity and
quiet cultivated by the chosen few in earlier centuries
cannot be recaptured, and even if the Industrial Revolution has not brought that perfection in humanity
which the nineteenth century hoped for, it has given to
the life of all a zip, a rush, a strenuous excitement,
a mad haste, from which there is no escape but
enjoyment.

BIBLIOGRAPHICAL NOTE

THE earliest conception of the Industrial Revolution as an English development of the latter eighteenth and earlier nineteenth centuries led to the making of the first inquiries into the nature of the movement by scholars in the field of English history; and the investigations of the English aspects of the subject still stand first in volume and diversity of special topics.

Among the more useful books giving a general view of the English experience are W. Cunningham, *The industrial revolution* (1908); C. R. Fay, *Great Britain from Adam Smith to the present day* (1928); J. L. and B. Hammond, *The rise of modern industry* (1925); L. C. A. Knowles, *The industrial and commercial revolutions in Great Britain in the nineteenth century* (1921), and *The economic development of the British over-seas empire* (1924); P. Mantoux, *The industrial revolution in the eighteenth century* (1928); G. H. Perris, *The industrial history of modern England* (1920); G. Slater, *The making of modern England* (1915); A. Toynbee, *Lectures on the industrial revolution of the eighteenth century in England* (1927); A. P. Usher, *The industrial history of England* (1920); C. Waters, *A short survey of the economic development of England and the colonies, 1874-1914* (1925); and J. H. Clapham, *An economic history of modern Britain* (1926). Of this important work only the first volume, covering the years 1820 to 1850, has appeared.

Somewhat more special studies suitable for further reading include G. D. H. Cole, *A short history of the British working class movement* (1925); Lord Ernle (R. E. Prothero), *English farming, past and present* (1919); W. T. Jackman, *The development of transportation in modern England* (1916); and S. and B. Webb, *The consumers' cooperative movement* (1921), and *The history of trade unionism* (1920).

Much of the best material for the other nations of Europe is naturally in foreign languages, including such general accounts as W. Sombart, *Die deutsche Volkswirtschaft im neunzehnten Jahrhundert* (1903); and A. Sartorius von Waltershausen, *Deutsche Wirtschaftsgeschichte* (1923), for German developments; M. Augé-Laribé, *Evolution de la France agricole* (1912); E. Levasseur, *Histoire des classes ouvrières et de l'industrie en France de 1789 à 1870* (1903-04); and H. See, *L'évolution commerciale et industrielle de la France sous L'ancien Régime* (1925), for the French story; J. Kulisher, *Russische Wirtschaftsgeschichte* (1925), for Russian economic history; and for the movement in Switzerland, W. E. Rappard, *La revolution industrielle et les origines de la protection legale du travail en Suisse* (1914).

Fortunately, the results of these and other volumes are summarized in a number of English works, such as J. H. Clapham, *The economic development of France and Germany, 1815-1914* (1921); W. H. Dawson, *Bismarck and state socialism* (1891), and *The evolution of modern Germany* (1914); and M. M. Knight, H. E. Barnes, and F. Flügel, *Economic history of Europe in modern times* (1928).

Denmark's progress is told in H. Westergaard, *Economic development in Denmark before and during the world war* (1922); and E. L. Bogart, *Economic history of the United States* (1920), and H. U. Faulkner, *American economic history* (1924), are among the most available treatments of the participation of the United States in the Industrial Revolution.

Students will find much to interest them in A. P. Usher, *A history of mechanical inventions* (1929); and the world-wide point of view of B. Harms, *Volkswirtschaft und Weltwirtschaft* is very provocative. The latest researches and monographs in English, German, French, and other lar‧guages, covering Europe in the modern period, are synthesized in J. Kulisher, *Allgemeine Wirtschaftsgeschichte,* vol. II, *Die Neuzeit* (1929).

INDEX